ANSWERS TO
PASTORS'
FAQs

ANSWERS TO
PASTORS'
FAQ~s~

HOWARD F. SUGDEN &
WARREN W. WIERSBE

NE✗GEN®

Building the New Generation of Believers

COOK COMMUNICATIONS MINISTRIES
Colorado Springs, Colorado • Paris, Ontario
KINGSWAY COMMUNICATIONS LTD
Eastbourne, England

NexGen® is an imprint of
Cook Communications Ministries, Colorado Springs, Colorado 80918
Cook Communications, Paris, Ontario
Kingsway Communications, Eastbourne, England

PASTORS' FAQs
© 2005 by SCRIPTEX, INC., WARREN W. WIERSBE, President
Revised and updated: original edition copyrighted © 1973 by Moody
Publishers, under the title *When Pastors Wonder How*; revised edition copyrighted © 1993 by Baker Book House Company, under the title *Confident Pastoral Leadership*.

First Printing, 2005
Printed in the United States of America

1 2 3 4 5 6 7 8 9 10 Printing/Year 10 09 08 07 06 05

Library of Congress Cataloging-in-Publication Data

Wiersbe, Warren W.
  Pastors' FAQ / Warren Wiersbe.-- [Rev. ed.].
    p. cm.
  Rev. ed. of: Confident pastoral leadership / Howard F. Sugden. 2nd ed. c1993.
  ISBN 0-7814-4156-0 (pbk.)
  1. Pastoral theology. I. Sugden, Howard F. Confident pastoral leadership. II. Title.
  BV4011.3.W54 2005
  253--dc22
                              2004026810

Contents

Preface to This Revision

It is difficult to believe that thirty years have passed since the first edition of this book was published. I rejoice that it has been in print all this time and that the response has been encouraging. For whatever help this book has been to those in pastoral ministry, I give thanks to the Lord. All the glory belongs to him.

I am not pastoring now, and my friend Howard Sugden has gone to be with our Lord. But our hearts have always been, and my heart remains, in the local church and with those who serve there. Many changes have taken place in the religious landscape during these thirty years, some encouraging and some frightening; but I have seen also that the inspired Word of God still meets the needs of God's people. "Preach the Word!" is still our mandate.

When my friends at Cook Communications/Victor Books suggested a new printing of this book, I suggested that we revise and expand it so that I might deal with some of the contemporary issues that the church faces. Cook Communications agreed, and the result is the volume you now hold in your hands. I want to thank my son David W. Wiersbe for his helpful suggestions. My editor Craig Bubeck was encouraging and patient as he waited for the manuscript.

If you are a young preacher, you may find this book quoting preachers from the past who are strangers to you. I urge you to get acquainted with them and to read their sermons and their biographies. They will enrich you. My book *Living with the Giants* (Baker) will introduce you to some of them and give you helpful bibliographies.

These are great days for ministry. May the Lord help us all to be faithful until he comes!

—Warren W. Wiersbe

Preface to the First Edition (1973)

God has called us to be pastors and to preach his Word, and, quite frankly, we enjoy it. Phillips Brooks put it beautifully in his *Lectures on Preaching*: "Let us rejoice with one another that in a world where there are a great many good and happy things for men to do, God has given us the best and happiest, and made us preachers of His Truth."

It has been our privilege to pastor small churches and large churches. At present, both of us are ministering in city churches. It has also been our privilege to minister in various conferences across the country. The most rewarding have often been the pastors' conferences where we have met with our brethren in the ministry and shared one another's burdens. Often we have conducted a question time when we have tried to encourage and to enlighten the brethren from the Word and from our own experience.

The questions and answers in this book have grown out of these seminars. It has often been suggested to us that we publish answers to the questions that have been asked most frequently, and this explains the publication of the book you are now reading. These questions deal primarily with the pastor and his work in the church. This is not a book about theological problems or Bible questions.

We do not expect every pastor to agree with every answer we have given. But we do expect our brethren to consider each answer honestly and ask for God's direction. We have not sprinkled these pages with "I remember a case when" and "Now, this is what happened to me." Pastors are busy people who appreciate answers that are to the point. No doubt every pastor can write his own illustrations from his own experience.

Please keep in mind that we wrote out of our own experience and therefore cannot speak with authority about every local church. Our own ministry has been spent in churches with independent ministries, though in fellowship with others of like faith. We realize that different denominations have different ways of handling matters, particularly in the areas of church discipline and calling pastors. The brethren pastoring in these churches can still, we think, benefit from what we have to say.

We must confess that we had young pastors in mind as we wrote these pages. For some reason, many of them are not taught these basic principles in school; and if we can save them some trouble and trials, we will feel amply repaid for our efforts. But the experienced pastor might be able to pick up a few new ideas or to be reminded of some forgotten principle. The man who boasts that he has fifteen years' experience in the ministry may not be telling the truth: perhaps he has had one year's experience—fifteen times.

We send this book forth with the prayer that it will assist and encourage our brethren in the ministry, so that we might all be effective in winning the lost and in building Christ's church.

—Howard F. Sugden and Warren W. Wiersbe

Chapter ONE

The Call to the Ministry

How can I know I'm called to the ministry and how important is the assurance of a special call?

The work of the ministry is too demanding and difficult for anyone to enter without a sense of divine calling. Too often people enter and then leave the ministry because they lack the sense of divine urgency that comes with a call. Nothing less than a definite call from God can ever give you success when the going gets tough in the ministry.

How do we know we are called? For some, there is a crisis experience—like those experienced by Moses at the burning bush or Isaiah in the temple or Paul on the Damascus Road. But for most of us there is simply that inescapable growing conviction that God has his hand upon us. Paul expressed it this way: "I am compelled to preach. Woe to me if I do not preach the gospel!" (see 1 Cor. 9:16). When you are called, you have an inner conviction that will not permit you to invest your life in any other vocation.

Along with this inner confidence there is the possession of the gifts and qualifications that God requires for his workers. The candidate for the ministry had better pray over and ponder the words of Paul in 1 Timothy 3:1–7 and Titus 1:5–9. No minister feels adequately equipped; even Paul exclaimed, "And who is equal to such a task?" (2 Cor. 2:16). But those who are truly called sense that God has given the spiritual gifts and natural abilities they need; these gifts and abilities must be dedicated, cultivated, and used for God's glory.

Certainly pastors must have character and conduct above reproach. They must sincerely desire to serve Christ and have a love for the Word and a desire to study it and share it with others. They must love people and be able to work well with them. They must have spiritual and emotional maturity. If married, the one called must be sure that the spouse agrees with the decision.

Along with this inner conviction, and an honest personal evaluation, must come approval from those who know the Lord. This doesn't mean that we must "confer with flesh and blood" (see Gal. 1:16 KJV) but it does mean that God's people will confirm what God has already said to us in our heart. If you feel you are called to preach, then begin to exercise your gifts in your local church and wherever else God gives you opportunities to serve. Spurgeon began his ministry by passing out tracts in tenement houses; D. L. Moody began as a Sunday school worker.

It's wise to spend time with a seasoned saint (preferably your pastor) to discuss these matters and to seek God's guidance. It's significant that, in the Bible, God preferred to call people who were busy: Gideon was threshing wheat; Moses was tending sheep; David was with his father's flock; Peter and Andrew were fishing. It is difficult to steer a car that's in neutral, and God usually doesn't guide a believer who is taking it easy.

Sometimes the church will sense God's call on a member's life even before the member senses it. John Knox was called to preach at the end of a sermon delivered by John Rough in Saint Andrew's Castle, when the preacher charged him solemnly "to refuse not this holy vocation." Knox ran to his room, wept and prayed, and finally came out obedient to the call. George W. Truett had a similar experience when he was challenged to the ministry by an old deacon in a Baptist church in Whitewright, Texas. Truett said, "I was thrown into the stream, and just had to swim!"

You shouldn't enter the ministry because you have failed at a dozen other jobs, or because there is nothing else to do. The oft-repeated counsel is worth repeating again: If you can stay out of the ministry, then do so. People who are God-called will know it, if they are sincerely yielded to God's will; nothing else will satisfy them but to do the will of God.

One word of warning: If you appear to have pastoral gifts but do not feel called to a full-time ministry, then get busy in your local church and use your gifts for God's glory, but don't try to pastor the church or to appoint yourself the unofficial assistant pastor. Faithful, gifted laymen who consider themselves "almost pastors" can be either a great help or a great hindrance in a local church. If they respect their pastor's divine call to be shepherd, they can be a great help in the ministry. If they decide to ignore pastoral authority, they can create no end of trouble, particularly if they think they are more gifted than the pastor God has called.

One final word of counsel: Give yourself time to discern God's will. This doesn't mean endless excuses and delays, for that approach indicates indecision and fear. Spend extra time in prayer and in the reading of God's Word. Some of the greatest preachers determined God's leading while they were busy in other occupations. G. Campbell Morgan was a teacher in a boys' school and used his extra hours to win lost souls. George Morrison served on the editorial staff of the great *Oxford English Dictionary* while seeking God's leading for his life. When you are quietly obedient in the everyday tasks of life, you will hear the voice of God and know which way to go.

Once I'm sure of my call, what do I do next?

If you're not already exercising your spiritual gifts in a local church, then get busy! First Timothy 3:6 warns that a pastor "must not be a recent convert." This suggests that ministerial candidates need a time of spiritual maturing under the supervision of leaders in the local church. The deacon must "first be tested" (1 Tim. 3:10), and this policy is also good for the ministerial candidate.

God's usual plan is to let his servants prove themselves faithful over a few things before he makes them rulers over many things (Matt. 25:21). Too much too soon can lead to "too bad too late." Spurgeon began as a Sunday school teacher. One Sunday he was asked to address the entire group because the leader was absent, and he was so successful that he eventually directed the school. Because Spurgeon was faithful to his little flock at Waterbeach in Cambridge, God gave him a great ministry in London. People who are not faithful in the little tasks will never have opportunity to prove themselves faithful in the big tasks. Start where you are; do what must be done; and let God open the way.

Perhaps the leaders of your church will want to license you to preach. A license to preach is to ordination what an engagement ring is to marriage: it's the first step, and it can always be revoked. Paul warns church leaders, "Do not be hasty in the laying on of hands" (1 Tim. 5:22). Before the church lays hands on you for ordination, be sure God has laid his hand on you for a lifetime of service (Phil. 3:12–14). It's better to be patient and certain than to be impetuous and embarrassed.

Start praying and planning for specialized training. Your pastor and other mature Christians can give you guidance concerning available schools. Please don't use the old excuse that many great preachers never went to school! Charles Spurgeon, Dwight L. Moody, H. A. Ironside, and G. Campbell Morgan never attended schools for pastoral training, yet two of them founded schools for preparing preachers and the other two sat on learned faculties. They knew the importance of education. If you are a Spurgeon or an Ironside, people will recognize it in a hurry; but until then, plan to get involved in training.

Watch out for the Devil's attacks during this waiting time. He often uses other Christians to discourage the would-be preacher, so maintain a strong devotional life in the Word and prayer. Be devoted to Christ; be disciplined; be busy. Claim Proverbs 3:5–6 and Psalm 37:3–5.

WHAT REALLY IS "ADEQUATE PREPARATION" FOR THE MINISTRY?

God has many ways of preparing his servants, and we should never despise or question his ways. He has a special purpose for each of his workers, and he alone knows how to prepare his tools. Keep your eyes on the Lord and not on other Christians, and let God work out his specific will for your life.

There is more than one kind of preparation for the ministry. There is, for example, *general preparation* that comes from daily living. Paul was a tentmaker, Peter and James and John were fishermen, and each of these men learned a great deal about life and people from their daily vocation. Many a practical lesson is learned in the office or factory, so never despise your hours of labor. Fortunate is the pastor who has learned by experience what it means to be a Christian in today's workaday world out there in the marketplace.

There is a trend today toward calling pastoral staff right out of the congregation, and in many churches this has worked well. The people called already know the church and the congregation and they don't have to relocate from another city. But it's wise for the church to provide a continuing education program so that these staff people can get the specialized training they may need.

Of course, there is *vocational preparation*, which includes studying the Word, acquiring a working knowledge of Bible languages, and gaining an understanding of Bible doctrine and church history. Practical training in Christian service is essential. "Able to teach" is one of the important qualifications for the ministry (1 Tim. 3:2) and it implies that a person is "able to learn." We must be receivers before we can be transmitters. People who fail to learn the discipline of study will never accomplish all God wants them to accomplish in the ministry. (See Ezra 7:6, 10.)

There are two major options available when it comes to formal education, and you and the Lord must decide which is best for you. You can spend four years in an accredited Bible institute or Christian college and then go to seminary, or you can earn an undergraduate degree at a secular college or university and then go to seminary. If you take the latter course, your best majors might be history, literature, or philosophy. Some will feel called to earn further graduate degrees, but be careful not to use school as an escape from the realities of the ministry. It is easy to die by degrees! If your undergraduate degree is in engineering or science, don't think this disqualifies you from ministry, because everything you study is useful in the Lord's service.

Whatever course of study you follow, be sure you graduate knowing how to use the basic tools of the ministry. A working knowledge of the Bible is fundamental. Try to get hold of the basics of the Bible languages, even though there are many useful language tools available and you should use them. Good courses in preaching are essential so that you learn to prepare and present organized messages from the Word. Your basic courses in theology will help you recognize heresy when you see it and will also keep you from confusion and contradiction in your preaching. History and philosophy may be dry, but they can give you perspective and depth.

You must be a student all your life. Everything that pastors experience or read can become a part of the spiritual treasury from which they can draw in the work of the Lord. You must major in the Book, but you will also read other books, both secular and sacred. You will read the book of nature and the book of humanity as well. As you live and learn, look for the places "where truth touches life" (Phillips Brooks), and there you will find the spiritual nourishment you need to feed your people.

To sum up: Trust God to lead you to the school that will best prepare you for the work he has called you to do. While you are there, give yourself devotedly to your studies, because you will never again have that same opportunity for preparation. Don't look upon formal education as a parenthesis or a detour in your life, but as part of your obedience to the will of God. Scholarship is stewardship. You minister to the Lord by being a good student as well as a good preacher, so be faithful. At some point you may be tempted to quit school and get out into the work. Resist this temptation! W. B. Riley says it so well: "If your work in school makes a student of you, one of the essential preparations for preaching will have been accomplished. If you leave school with no love of study, the background of school will be of little value" (*The Preacher and His Preaching* [Wheaton, Ill.: Sword of the Lord, 1948] 21).

DOES GOD CALL PEOPLE PERMANENTLY TO THE MINISTRY?

"No one who puts his hand to the plow and looks back is fit for service in the kingdom of God" (Luke 9:62). The emphasis throughout the Bible is on a permanent call. Please don't enter the ministry with reservations or with a hidden agenda. It is unwise to ask God for an escape clause in the contract. The couple that enters marriage saying, "Well, if it doesn't work, we can always get a divorce" is asking for trouble, and so is the pastor who says to himself, "If I don't make it, I can always get a different job." Ministry is a calling, not a job, unless you are a hireling (John 10:11–13). "For God's gifts and his call are irrevocable" (Rom. 11:29). People who are called but try to run away will, like Jonah, discover that there is no place to hide.

This doesn't mean that God never changes a servant's sphere of ministry. Many a faithful pastor has been led from the local church ministry into teaching, missionary work, Bible-conference ministry, or denominational responsibilities. Sometimes a crisis in the home requires a change of ministry. Some pastors have had to change their sphere of service in order to help care for an invalid spouse or aged parents.

Every servant of God has, at one time or another, sensed a personal inadequacy for the work of the ministry. "No day passes," wrote the great Marcus Dods in his diary, "without strong temptation to give up, on the ground that I am not fitted for pastoral work. Writing sermons is often the hardest labor; visiting is terrible." Yet Dods became a great force for God, and pastors still read his books and benefit from them.

If an hour of depression comes, and you feel like giving up, don't do it. God has called you, God is with you, and God is going to use you to accomplish his purposes. Get alone with God; instead of resigning from the work, re-sign your commission and get back to work. "Being confident of this, that he who began a good work in you will carry it on to completion until the day of Christ Jesus" (Phil. 1:6).

SHOULD OLDER PEOPLE CONSIDER A CALL TO MINISTRY?

Why not? There seems to be little evidence that the call of God comes only to young people. Amos and Moses were settled in their vocations when God called them to preach. In fact, older people have advantages that younger ministerial candidates may not possess: experience in life, seriousness of purpose, a maturity that formal education alone can never impart, a sense of values, a sense of perspective, and a deeper understanding of human nature. Many educators claim that their older students do far better than the younger ones, if only because they have to try harder.

Of course, older candidates have some special problems to overcome: the high cost of starting a new vocation in midlife, the ever-rolling stream of time, a measure of financial security, the difficulty of becoming a student again and having to sit in class with younger people, and just the pain of pulling up roots and relocating. But these so-called stumbling blocks can become stepping-stones for the person who believes God. The important thing is not your age but your willingness to obey God regardless of the cost. More and more people these days are being called into ministry in midlife and must make midcourse adjustments, so don't think you're alone in this vocational transition.

In many respects, age is a state of mind. Cultivate the faith outlook on life, and you will always be young in heart and spirit. We once read a desk motto: "Growing old is nothing but a bad habit which a busy person has no time to acquire."

WHAT PART DOES ONE'S SPOUSE PLAY IN A CALL TO THE MINISTRY?

A very important part! The spouse must be a help and not a hindrance. A sovereign God, knowing he will call a person into his service, will also direct that person to choose a spouse who will be an agreeable and encouraging helper. The problems of the ministry are great enough without adding to them the burden of a divided household. If an engaged couple doesn't agree on the call to service, then let them break the engagement, pray for God's direction and wait until there is peace and confidence in both hearts. "Do two walk together unless they have agreed to do so?" (Amos 3:3).

The man or woman already married faces a more difficult problem. But if the wife is a good homemaker and a loving mate, there should be no problem; the pastor's wife is first a keeper of the home. She need not be a stirring banquet speaker, a gifted musician, or a successful teacher to be a good pastor's wife. If she can keep the home running smoothly so that her husband can fulfill his ministry, she will accomplish the most important task. The wife sensing a call to ministry must work these matters out with her husband, perhaps with the help of a counselor, so that she and her husband are a team and not in competition.

Let the wife talk and pray with some experienced "mother in Israel" before she decides whether she is truly called to ministry. There must be agreement and harmony in the home. But this should be true of all Christian homes, not just the homes of full-time Christian workers; so if a call to the ministry brings about violent reactions in the marriage, something may be radically wrong with its basic structure. Better that these things are worked out lovingly and patiently before too many changes are made, preferably under the guidance of a mature pastor. A married couple must consider their children as well (1 Tim. 5:8) and not upset the home. God doesn't usually tear one thing down in order to build another thing up.

When marriage vows precede ordination vows, the laying on of hands doesn't automatically cancel the marriage vows. If the husband and wife feel they have married in the will of God, then let them wait on the Lord until they are sure that the call to ministry is of the Lord. To conclude that full-time ministry is impossible is to limit the grace and power of God. It's especially important that the children in the home be prepared for what to them will be a radical change. Time plus wise counsel and God's grace can help to smooth out the problems. If there is still no agreement, let the couple keep the marriage together and find outlets for their gifts in their local church. David wanted to build a temple for the Lord but God assigned the task to his son Solomon. God's words to David encourage all of us: "Because it was in your heart … you did well to have this in your heart" (2 Chron. 6:8).

I AM A MINISTRY "DROPOUT." HOW CAN I GET BACK INTO SERVICE?

After much heart-searching and prayer, start counseling with a pastor you know and trust. Some of the questions you must answer honestly are: Why did I drop out? Have the problems been solved? Am I now in the place of God's blessing so he can use me again? Have I taken the necessary steps to repair any damage I have done? Are there any character weaknesses that need to be dealt with before I can pastor again? How does my spouse see the situation?

John Mark was a dropout, and God restored him and used him greatly. Even the great apostle Paul had to change his opinion about Mark (read Acts 15:36–41; Col. 4:10; 2 Tim. 4:11). Both Jonah and Peter failed in their calling, yet God forgave them and restored them. "So he made it again another vessel" (Jer. 18:1–4 KJV).

Rest on God's Word, not the opinions of men. David expressed a great truth when, after he had sinned, he said, "Let me fall into the hands of the LORD, for his mercy is very great; but do not let me fall into the hands of men" (1 Chron. 21:13). Sometimes the responses of other pastors to your situation can be very discouraging and condemning, but God has promised to forgive (1 John 1:9) and to restore repentant believers to fellowship and blessing. Rest on his promises!

Don't jump into the first opportunity for service that comes your way. Be sure you serve in the place of God's choosing. You can't afford another crisis and failure. Perhaps working with an experienced pastor for a time would help you transition back into service. "Watch and pray!" Satan is out to defeat and devour all of us. It's not necessary to assume that you will fail again; in fact, a defeatist attitude will assure such failure. But it is necessary to heed 1 Corinthians 10:12.

Chapter TWO

The Call to a Church

What steps should I take in finding a place to minister?

Ephesians 2:10 indicates that God prepares us for what he has prepared for us; so, if we're called of the Lord, he has a place chosen where we can serve successfully. Most pastors start in a smaller place, and then God leads them into larger fields of ministry. A few are called into large spheres almost from the beginning, but this is not God's usual procedure (Matt. 25:21). We start as the servants of a few and, if we're faithful, God will enlarge our sphere of ministry.

We assume that you have been serving the Lord in some way during your years of preparation, and that from this experience you have discovered and developed your gifts and abilities. "Know thyself" is an important admonition for ministers of the Word if they would not find themselves in the wrong place doing the wrong job.

Cultivate a servant's heart and be available. Never look upon any assignment or opportunity as small and unworthy. It has well been said, "Make every occasion a great occasion, for you can never tell when someone may be taking your measure for a larger place." People who are too proud to preach to a small congregation will never preach successfully to large congregations. Joshua got his start as Moses' servant, and David killed the lion and the bear in private before God permitted him to slay the giant in public. If you are called and prepared, then keep busy and trust God until he opens the right door for you.

It would be helpful if you could work for a year or two with an experienced minister, not to imitate but to learn and to confirm your call. Serving as an assistant pastor may not have the glamour found in shepherding your own flock, but it does present several advantages. An experienced pastor will teach you and cover for you when you make mistakes. This arrangement is also good for your family as they move gradually into pastoral work. During a few years of assisting in ministry, you can develop your study habits and pastoral skills. As a spectator at church business meetings, you can learn a great deal about the dynamics of church leadership. If your senior pastor includes you in the church councils on occasion, be careful to keep confidence at all times.

If no door of ministry opens immediately, don't give up. The great Bible scholar Marcus Dods, whom we mentioned before, waited for six years before a church called him. During that time he ministered as a guest preacher, studied, prepared messages and waited for God's time. When the door finally opened, it led into a lifetime of fruitful service.

God sometimes uses other people to direct us into his will. Let some of your pastor friends know you're open to God's leading, and perhaps they can make suggestions. Often churches contact other pastors when they are seeking a shepherd; while we don't lean on the arm of flesh, we do permit God to use other believers to give us guidance along the way.

The worst thing you can do is promote yourself and try to push your way into some choice pulpit. To use denominational politics to secure a call is to give evidence that you have no confidence in the promises of God or in the power of prayer. Faith is living without scheming; the sooner the new pastor learns this, the better. Nehemiah "prayed to the God of heaven, and ... answered the king" (Neh. 2:4–5), and that's the correct order. If you are walking with God, he will lead you to the right friends and to the right place of ministry.

These suggestions apply primarily to pastors in fellowships or denominations in which the local churches are free to call their own ministers. Those belonging to denominations that operate differently will perhaps find little help in these suggestions. Our own experience has been in the independent tradition, and we hesitate to give counsel outside the sphere of our own experience.

WHAT SHOULD WE DO WHEN WE'RE INTERVIEWED BY A PULPIT COMMITTEE?

Usually the members of the committee have already heard you preach, so you are not a stranger to them. They should also have studied your résumé. Go to the meeting with a warm, loving spirit and ask God to give you wisdom and direction (James 1:5). Determine to be a blessing and all will go well.

The purpose of the meeting, of course, is for the church leaders to get acquainted with you and for you to get better acquainted with the church, its leaders and its ministry. Here are some guidelines to follow:

Before the meeting

Both husband and wife should read whatever material is available about the church, its history, and its program. Especially informative are the church constitution and bylaws, as well as copies of recent budgets and annual reports. If no reports are available, write out the pertinent questions that you want to ask about finances. If you come with a set of significant questions, you will help to keep the meeting on target and save a great deal of time and energy. Of course, the chairperson of the meeting ought to have a definite agenda, but not every chairperson knows this. It's wise to be prepared.

During the meeting

The committee will want to hear your personal testimony and any report of your ministry you can give. They may ask you for references, so be prepared with a list of names and addresses. Be sure to listen carefully and to answer every question in a loving Christian way, even if the question appears rude or critical. This first contact with the key people of the church ought to be on a high level; for, if you become their pastor, you already have begun well. Be sure that every area is covered, and don't be ashamed to discuss finances. Take notes! This will save misunderstanding and embarrassment later. Ask the committee to explain any matters of church ministry that are not clear to you. You have every right to know "the state of the union."

Don't make an impetuous decision to accept or to reject the call at this preliminary meeting. Be sure to leave the meeting with a wholesome attitude, and thank the committee members for their time and their help.

After the meeting

It's up to the committee to make a statement to you by letter, either asking you to consider the church or informing you that they will be looking elsewhere. It's tragic when committees are so thoughtless that they fail to inform the candidate of their decision. If they invite you to consider the church, it's wise to return to the field, preach several times, and take more time to meet the people and consider the situation. "He that believeth shall not make haste" (Isa. 28:16 KJV). Be sure all the details relating to the call are clearly spelled out in a formal letter: salary, housing, moving expenses (which the church should pay), responsibilities, vacation privileges. It is better to have these defined in advance than debated on arrival.

Certainly you will spend much time in prayer, seeking the mind of the Lord. Feel free to contact the committee chairperson if you need to discuss any matter. Even if the church doesn't call you, this experience can be a means of spiritual growth, and it might open other doors. If no call comes, don't become resentful. It may take time for people to recognize how gifted we are! Continue to pray for the church, that God will send them the minister of his choice.

Perhaps a few don'ts are in order:

- Don't major on minors in the discussions. Keep to the basics.
- Don't argue with the committee about anything. If the members are not biblical in some matter, you can state your case lovingly; don't turn the meeting into a debate.
- Don't expect everything to be perfect. Churches are made up of people, and people are human and fallible. So are people who are preachers! Only God never makes mistakes.
- Don't criticize the church, the public services, or the building. These people love their church, and you should love it, too, warts and all.
- Don't resent being looked upon as a beginner. Some of the committee members have been around a long time and have interviewed many pastoral candidates. If at first they don't recognize your maturity, be patient; if the gifts are there, God will make them known in his good time.
- Don't make the mistake of thinking that all pulpit committees are alike. You will meet cautious committees, afraid to step out by faith; divided committees that don't know what kind of pastor the church needs; and weary committees, ready to call the first candidate they meet. Give yourself time to sense the atmosphere of the meeting, and you will come away feeling at peace.

Trust God to use the committee and to give you all the guidance you need. Committee members will make mistakes; they will display prejudices and perhaps even ignorance, but God is still on the throne and your trust is in him. It's possible that they may return to you after considering other candidates, but don't hold your breath. Keep serving and trusting the Lord to work out his perfect plan in your life. God's timing is always best, and our "times are in [his] hands" (Ps. 31:15).

How can I know that God has called me to minister to a specific congregation?

During your first contacts with the congregation of God's choice, he may put into your heart the conviction that you "belong" with these people. More than one candidate has said, "I felt like I'd been in the church all my life." There will be a peace in your heart, and as you pray, the conviction will deepen. You will have a burden for the work and sense an excitement as you anticipate sharing in it. If you are moving from another pastorate, you may experience a lifting of the burden from that work and a growing burden for the new work. This may happen over a period of time, or it may come suddenly. Usually, there is a time of preparation when God weans the pastor and the family away from one church and directs them into another work. Remember, you don't leave a place—you go to a place.

The possibilities—yes, even the problems—of the prospective pastorate will challenge you. The existence of serious problems in a work is no reason to leave it (Titus 1:5 settles that), and neither is it a reason to avoid it. You do not have to agree totally with the organization and the structure of a church in order to be its pastor. Perhaps God has called you there to set something in order in due time. Of course, you and the church ought to agree doctrinally.

Most pastors like to talk over these decisions with pastor friends whom they love and trust, but don't talk to too many people. Share your decisions with your most trusted counselors and pray together for God's direction. Often, other Christians who know and love us will ratify the leading God gives us in our own hearts.

Never accept a church because there's no other place to go, or because you have problems in your present ministry. Unsolved problems in the former ministry have a way of appearing in the new ministry. Ministers who hop from church to church never mature in the ministry; they keep running from the very challenges that can help them grow. Pastors who relocate because of problems in their present churches are like adolescents who get married just to get away from home, only to discover bigger problems in the new place.

These big decisions of life are often built upon the little decisions that we make day after day; so keep your devotional life at a high level, and God will show you his will.

SHOULD I ACCEPT A CALL IF THE VOTE HAS NOT BEEN UNANIMOUS?

Alas, some churches don't have the word "unanimous" in their vocabulary. In fact, many churches (sad to say) have a few sanctified obstructionists in their membership whose purpose in life is to keep the church from ever having a unanimous vote on anything.

Your decision should be influenced by the size of the negative vote. Wisdom dictates that there should be a comfortable majority to work with; but opposition does present a challenge to a true servant of God. In fact, some who voted for you may turn against you before you have been on the field very long; and some of your opponents may become your most loyal workers. If the negative vote is small, you can accept the call with safety in God's will. But if there is a sizable and vocal minority, it is wise to wait.

Many churches take the vote, and if the majority agrees on a call, they then make the vote unanimous. This is a standard procedure, but it leaves the new pastor thinking that the church is united when it may not be. You have a right to know whether or not there was a considerable negative vote.

If you accept the call, don't try to find out how people voted. Some will say to you, "Well, I voted against you, so be careful!" Treat all of the people graciously and seek to win their love and confidence. Pastor the whole church, not just your admirers. One day you will have the joy of seeing the church happily united, including the people who voted against you.

Some pastors feel they have failed unless every vote is a unanimous one. If you have this attitude, you will lose much joy in the ministry. A pastor and his people must seek the Lord's direction and vote as they feel led. The majority must rule, and the minority must disagree without being disagreeable. If the majority is right, it must not adopt a "we-are-God's-people" attitude. If the minority turns out to be right, it must not say, "We told you so!" The pastor's personal attitude in these matters is the key to church harmony and progress. If he becomes dictatorial, he will divide the church. If he exercises love and patience, he will unite the church.

Chapter THREE

The Pastor in a New Church

---

*How do I get started right in a new place
of ministry?*

Begin by daily asking God to give you a deepening love for your people. Get to know them; build a prayer list and faithfully remember your people before the throne of grace.

Get acquainted enthusiastically with the work of the church. Avoid criticism; there are two sides (or more) to every story, so don't believe everything you hear. Learn to appreciate the people, the buildings, the traditions, even though later you may be led to make changes. Be wary of people who obviously want to become your confidants. In a few months, they could become your enemies. Especially beware of quickly accepting former members who return and want to immediately become active. Get the facts first and note that Titus 3:10 sets a limit to how often people can leave in anger and return with a smile.

As you get acquainted with the work, make a list of personal priorities, the important things you would like to accomplish. You can't do everything at once, and some things, when they're accomplished, will make it easier to perform other tasks. Turn this list of priorities into a prayer list. Ask God to give you the wisdom to understand the situation and to know when to begin to act.

Be patient. It is amazing what can be accomplished with patience and prayer. Some pastors think they must have record accomplishments during the first month of their ministry, and they begin *driving* the sheep instead of *leading* them. Ask God for patience and understanding.

Try to avoid comparing your new place of ministry with the one you just left. It's difficult to plow a straight furrow when you're looking back. Each situation is different because God's people are all different. Principles of ministry never change, but methods do change from place to place. If you constantly compare one church with another, you may gradually become critical, and a critical pastor has a hard time loving and serving the people.

Visit your people, especially the elderly, the shut-ins, and the church leaders. The elderly will appreciate your visits, and their loved ones will thank you for caring. These people may be among the first to die and it is good to know them before you conduct the funeral. The shut-in members and friends may be your greatest prayer partners. And it's good to be in the homes of church leaders, because knowledge of their homes will help you in understanding the people themselves. You may be more patient with a deacon when you discover the burdens he bears at home.

Preach heartening messages from the great passages in the Word. Many preachers prefer to preach through a book or in an announced series. This approach disarms the critical members who want to accuse you of preaching against certain sins in the church. If controversial topics (e.g., divorce or church divisions) do come up, critics cannot accuse you of selecting your topics and taking unfair advantage from the pulpit.

Take advantage of your newness to visit as many people as possible. "I'm the new pastor at First Church!" is a key to open doors for several months, but eventually you will have to hang up the key and take a new approach. Consult with your official board and find out if they advise you to visit members who have dropped out. By all means visit the unsaved and try to win them to Christ. This may include the parents of Sunday school children. The "visiting pastor" may be a rarity today and the experts ridicule the old saying that "a home-going pastor means a church-going people," but your ministry from the pulpit will be more personal if you take time to visit in the homes. Pastoral visitation is sometimes ignored and even criticized by some preachers, and we readily acknowledge the fact that visiting today may not be as effective as it was years ago, but we still feel that pastors will learn much and do a better job if they get to know their people.

However, "getting to know the people" doesn't mean listening to all sorts of criticism of former pastors and other church members. We repeat: don't believe everything you hear. In fact, when people start to criticize, gently ask them to stop. In time, word will get around that the new pastor does not encourage gossip. This doesn't mean you should turn a deaf ear to a trusted officer who wants to warn you about a persistent problem person. But it does mean you don't categorize people on the basis of the prejudices of a few members. The family that didn't respond to the last pastor's ministry may respond when they hear you preach. You will hear both good and bad about many people. Don't commit yourself. Allow God to direct you, and ponder Proverbs 18:13.

You don't demand respect; you command it. Your people want to love you and follow you, but they need time to get to know you. Once you have won their love and respect, they will be willing to follow your leadership. Quietly go to work winning the lost, organizing the work, building the saints, and moving the church into wider ministries. In time, God's blessing will win for you the respect and the cooperation you desire.

Plan to stay. Your desire to stay with the people, in spite of their faults (and yours), will endear you to them. Let it be known that you want to do a solid work in the church and not merely visit them for a year or so "until something better opens up."

Pray regularly for your leaders by name. Ask God to make them spiritual. Let them know privately that you pray for them, and ask them to share their special needs with you.

When that first crisis comes, face it and handle it as though you had been in the church for ten years. Exercise love and kindness, and obey the Word of God. The way you do things the first time will determine the way you do them the second and the third time. Once your people realize that you mean to obey God's Word, most people will respond with appreciation and cooperation. Others will either pout or leave.

As your plans crystallize, talk them over privately with your leaders. They have a right to know where you're leading the church. Don't pressure them into moving quickly. Pressured people usually respond negatively. Instead, "be calm in thy soul." Where there's calmness and a sense of direction, people will respond positively. It takes time to build a spiritual church, so don't become frustrated if things don't change overnight. Good beginnings usually mean good endings, so watch your beginnings.

Stay close to home that first year on the field. Once you've established yourself in your ministry, you will have opportunities to minister in other places from time to time. But don't become a guest speaker in your own pulpit.

Get to know the other pastors in your area. Some of them will become your closest friends and will remain friends after you leave that field. Be friendly to all, even those with whom you may disagree. You may not want them in your pulpit, but don't exclude them from your friendship and prayers.

I FEEL GOD HAS CALLED ME TO A SPECIFIC CHURCH, BUT THERE ARE THINGS ABOUT THE WORK THAT DESPERATELY NEED CHANGING. HOW DO I GO ABOUT MAKING CHANGES?

Pastors who feel they must agree with everything in the church program before they will accept a call are doomed to disappointment and defeat in the ministry. Of course, there must be agreement in basic doctrine and polity, but it isn't necessary for us to feel that everything must be done our way before God can bless. Many good pastors will tell you after years of ministry in one church that some situations and policies still haven't changed, yet they've been able to minister with blessing.

The successful change agent must have authority, stature, strategy, faith, and patience. You were given authority when the church called you and installed you as their shepherd, but to minister only on the basis of authority is to *drive* the flock, not *lead* it, and when sheep are driven, they get afraid and start to scatter. You were *given* authority as a leader but you must *earn* stature by being a servant and by winning the hearts of your people. Phillips Brooks said that a minister must be a preacher to have authority and a pastor to have sympathy, and he was correct. The loving pastor eventually gains the stature needed to guide the flock successfully.

Begin by creating an atmosphere of love and confidence. This takes time, prayer, and a great deal of sacrifice. If you are a servant of the people for Jesus' sake, you soon will become their leader. As we mentioned before, we do not demand respect; we command it. Commanding respect involves love, time, and occasional pain.

Build your strategy as the Lord directs you. Without strategy, you don't know where you're going or how to respond to the opposition that is bound to come. Distinguish between your own pet desires and the real needs of the church. If you make changes only to suit yourself, you are being selfish and shortsighted. Changes should be made in order to make the church more spiritual and to improve the ministry of the congregation. Change for the sake of change is novelty, and you can't build a strong work on novelty. Nor can you afford to be experimenting constantly. As we suggested before, have a list of priorities and let them be your guide. Make as few changes as possible, and be sure they are basic and not merely surface changes. Also, make sure they are biblical.

It is often good policy to ask the church to try things out for a short time. If the trial works, fine; if not, nothing is lost. People are usually willing to try something if they are not committed for life. We are fallible creatures and it is possible for even the godliest leader to make a mistake.

Timing is important, so be patient. Try for "order in the midst of change and change in the midst of order" (Alfred North Whitehead). Remember that you're making changes for the good of the ministry, not for the glory of the minister.

Win the confidence of the people first, introduce your plans with

"We ought" or "Perhaps we should" rather than "You should" or "God told me," and be careful of giving the impression that you are carrying a big stick. If the sheep are fed, they may be led; but sheep do not like to be driven.

How does the pastor become the leader in the church?

Pastors become leaders by accepting their calling as leaders with humility and by using their office for the good of others and the glory of God. The church does not make the pastor the leader; God does (2 Cor. 4:5). The Lord Jesus Christ was a great pastor: "He goes on ahead of them, and his sheep follow him because they know his voice" (John 10:4).

Read 1 Peter 5 and John 13:17, and let these principles of spiritual leadership burn themselves into your soul. We lead by loving people and manifesting humility, not by demanding what we want and forcing people to obey. We lead by setting the example. We've heard of pastors who at the first business meeting announce that the church constitution is being set aside and the pastor will become the constitution. As Dr. E. K. Bailey used to say, "The only thing they will change is their address." The Pharisees were harder on the people than they were on themselves, but not so the New Testament pastor. Before we preach, we must practice what we preach.

We lead through the Word of God and prayer. When the sheep are fed, they are usually happy to follow. We lead through sacrificial service (read Phil. 2), by paying a price. John Henry Jowett said that ministry that costs nothing accomplishes nothing. He was right.

We lead "in season and out of season." In our personal friendly conversations with our people, as well as in church business meetings, we show that we can be trusted, that we don't argue and that we listen to others without interrupting. The casual conversation with an officer you meet in the supermarket might be more effective than next Sunday's sermon, if the Lord is in it!

We lead by carrying responsibility and being faithful to do our work, accepting a lot more of the blame and a lot less of the praise. Being early to appointments, always having an agenda, giving credit where credit is due, and admitting mistakes are ways to win the respect of the people.

We pastors need to remember that our people have had different experiences with former pastors, and some of those experiences may have left wounds. Some church members will be cautious when it comes to accepting and following a new pastor. Here is where patience and love come in.

How can you tell when you are finally moving into the place of spiritual leadership that you desire?

For one thing, the machinery of the church will speed up and move smoothly. There will still be opposition—and loyal opposition has its place in congregational government—but opposition will not be a threat. The people will be open to your suggestions. It's a good sign when church members can feel free to disagree with their pastor and do so with the right spirit. You will start to feel at home in the administrative work of the church. You will find yourself understanding the hearts and the minds of your leaders and you will be better able to work with them. At the same time, they will have a clearer idea of your plans and your style of leadership and will be eager to listen and to work with you.

The privilege of leadership must never be exploited for personal gain. Authority must always be exercised for the good of the church and the glory of God. "The chief is servant of all," says an African proverb. Jesus said, "The greatest among you will be your servant" (Matt. 23:11). As you grow in your leadership abilities, you will also gain in leadership opportunities. God does not want you or the church to stand still; so, with increased leadership will come increased opportunities for ministry. New opportunities will bring new demands, new challenges, and new problems; but this is far better than constantly facing the same old problems and getting nothing done. If each board agenda is only a carbon copy of previous agendas, something is radically wrong. Growing, cutting-edge churches face new challenges and new problems.

Stop at the nearest library or bookstore and check the books available on executive leadership and related themes. Sometimes the children of this world are wiser in these things than are the children of light, but always balance men's ideas with God's wisdom. The book of Nehemiah shows a true leader at work, and 2 Corinthians gives you insight into the heart of Paul as he faced and solved church problems. Read James 3:13–4:17 for insight into the two kinds of wisdom that can direct the work of a local church. Only God's wisdom is acceptable.

HOW IMPORTANT IS A CHURCH CONSTITUTION? WHAT'S THE BEST APPROACH TO MAKING CHANGES IN AN ANTIQUE CONSTITUTION THAT SUPPORTS A MINISTRY OUT OF STEP WITH WHAT THE LORD WANTS TO DO?

All things should be done decently and in order. The main purpose of a constitution is to insure order. Many churches are incorporated, and by law require a constitution and a set of bylaws. But even if a church is not legally incorporated, it needs organizational guidelines or else its activities will create chaos.

Some churches mistakenly think that a good constitution makes a good church. They try to cover every possible emergency and need and thus create a monster. The constitution is the track on which the train runs; it is not the steam in the boiler. One well-known pastor accepted the call of a famous church on the condition that they "put the constitution away for a whole year and use only the Bible in governing the church." However, the average pastor probably doesn't have the stature that man had; so you had better learn to live with the constitution until you are able to make the changes that ought to be made.

The constitution cannot make the church spiritual any more than the Ten Commandments could make Israel spiritual. Legalism is always a danger, particularly in groups that want to have high standards for their church. But adding or deleting articles in the constitution will never change the church. Changes can improve or hinder the organizational working of the church, but they can never change the hearts of the people. God alone can foster spirituality through the Spirit using the Word.

Be sure to read the church constitution carefully before accepting a church. If you have problems with some of the articles, discuss the matter freely with the official committee. Sometimes it's a matter of interpretation rather than principle. If God leads you to accept the church, live with the constitution and respect it, but begin to pray and plan for changes that you feel are really important. Be sure, however, that you're operating from a position of leadership before you suggest any changes, and give the people opportunity to pray and think things through. If your preaching and pastoral work have created an atmosphere of love and trust, the church will be willing to consider your ideas. Be sure you can back up your suggestions with the principles of the Word, but expect to find a few members who feel that the constitution is as inspired as the Bible. Furthermore, church members sometimes feel that pastors tamper with the church constitution only because they want more power and to "run the church" their way. Sometimes this is true, but it should not be true in your ministry.

If a church is repeatedly voting on new articles, members become frustrated and weary of the whole matter. Give yourself time to read and digest the whole constitution, decide with your leaders what changes really must be made, and take care of surgery all at once. Be a Christian statesman in the whole matter, and don't split your church over issues that aren't important. If you discover something disagreeable after coming to the church—something you could have known about before coming—please don't vent your anger on the church. Commit the matter to God; pray about it; and at the right time, discuss it with your leaders.

No matter what the form of church government, the pastor should be the spiritual leader of the congregation. First Peter 5:1–3, Hebrews 13:7, 1 Thessalonians 5:12, and 1 Timothy 3:5 seem to indicate this.

There are many areas within the church organization where gifted men and women will exercise better leadership than the pastor, but the flock should be under the pastor's direction. This doesn't mean that the senior minister must preside at every meeting. Our experience in the ministry has been with independent local churches where the pastor is the moderator of most church meetings, but we recognize that a gifted layperson could be moderator without usurping the God-given responsibilities or authority of the pastor. If your conviction is that the pastor should always preside, and the church considering you has a different arrangement, then you owe it to the church and to yourself to examine the matter carefully. You may create constant friction unless there is some mutual understanding.

I DISLIKE COMMITTEE MEETINGS. I'M REQUIRED TO ATTEND, SO HOW CAN I DEVELOP A BETTER ATTITUDE TOWARD THIS PART OF MY WORK?

Don't make the mistake of considering some parts of your work "spiritual" and other parts "organizational" or "administrative," because there is no such division. No matter what kind of meeting you're attending—a prayer meeting or a business meeting—you're pastoring the church. Once you begin to wear more than one hat (pastor and administrator), you will start to have headaches in both heads!

The church is an organization, but the church is also an organism; and if an organism is not organized, it will die. Paul's example in Acts and his teachings in the Epistles indicate that he believed in establishing local churches in an organized way. When organization becomes an end in itself and not a means to an end, then the church has become institutional and starts to die. Organization is to the church what the scaffolding is to a building under construction: it helps get the job done.

So, your first step is to get the right perspective on meetings that involve managing the important machinery of the church. Look upon these meetings as opportunities to pastor your leaders and help them grow spiritually. Never attend a committee meeting looking like someone expecting an execution. Approach the meeting in the fullness of the Spirit and with a desire to apply the Word of God to living situations. Sometimes you will accomplish more good in the life of a member by your words in a committee meeting than you would by your words from the pulpit. The organizational functions of the church are opportunities for you to practice what you preach—and perhaps that's what makes them seem so dreadful.

Maintain a close relationship with your key leaders. Your personal ministry to them as a pastor-friend will help establish wholesome relationships in public meetings. This doesn't mean that you should try to politick outside the business meetings, because such a practice is unwise. It does mean that you should develop a warm, loving relationship with your leaders so that you can all discuss matters and even disagree without becoming enemies.

Some pastors like to spend a day with church officers at their places of employment, just to get a better feel for what they do and what they face each day.

There's an art to chairing a meeting which, alas, some church officers have never had the opportunity to learn, so gradually teach them. Remind them that a good meeting always starts on time, has a prepared agenda, stays on target, and ends on time. "Work expands to fill the amount of time available for it." Give the average committee three hours for a meeting and its members will consume all three hours. Give them thirty minutes and they will probably be able to reach the same conclusions in thirty minutes. It takes time, but church leaders can be taught how to conduct an effective business meeting and get things done. But don't do your correcting in public unless absolutely necessary. Talk to problem people privately; they will appreciate your kindness.

G. Campbell Morgan followed a policy of "the minimum of organization for a maximum of work." It pays to examine your organizational structure at least once a year (some churches have this written into the constitution) to see if some of the scaffolding can be taken down. Be slow to create new committees; use existing organizations as long as they're healthy and function well.

Prayer lubricates the machinery of the church. It's been our experience that business meetings (and their length) decrease as prayer increases. Be sure to meet regularly with your officers for times of prayer. Pray about specific needs in the church and plans you have for the future. You will be surprised at what the Spirit will do.

It takes time for a new pastor to get acquainted with the machinery of the church. It also takes time for any pastor to develop leadership abilities. Don't permit mistakes or hurts from the past to hinder you from having a happy ministry today. Watch out for that conditioned reflex many pastors experience when their ideas are rejected. Learn to lose graciously and seek for win/win decisions. Chances are that some member of the board will remember your idea, think about it, present it at a future meeting as his or her own idea—and it will be accepted. There's no limit to what pastors can accomplish if they don't care who gets the credit. If God has directed you to the church and burdened you to accomplish certain things, then he will see you through if you will just be loving and patient. You may lose a few battles, but eventually you will win the war.

BECAUSE OF SOME PAST SCANDALS AND PROBLEMS, THE CHURCH I PASTOR HAS A BAD NAME IN OUR COMMUNITY. HOW DO I GO ABOUT RESTORING THE GOOD NAME OF THE CHURCH?

Thanks to the media, news coverage is faster and wider and people who enjoy wallowing in scandalous news rejoice in this. Alas, we're living in a time of religious reproach and people are suspicious and critical of what ministers and churches are doing. When scandal hits a local ministry and the facts are known, it hurts even more. Be a good Christian servant in the community and the people will take notice. In fact, they will probably give thanks that you're there, for a church with a bad name can't help but bring embarrassment. The fine people of your community will be behind you if you serve faithfully, so take heart. Some of them will admire you for taking on a tough assignment and will quietly support your work.

Find out how much of the past still lingers in the church. Work with individuals patiently and "pray out the poison." Ask God to help you create a sweet, loving spirit in the church, for "love covers over a multitude of sins" (1 Peter 4:8; see also Prov. 10:12). Word soon will get out that something new and exciting is happening in the congregation, and the contrast will be good promotion for you.

In the public services and the various official meetings, encourage your people to be positive about their church. "Forgetting what is behind" (Phil. 3:13) ought to be the motto of the congregation. As you teach the Word, it will cleanse and renew the people. We have said it before: Be patient and prayerful and give God time to work.

Finally, use advertising judiciously. Notices in the newspapers will let people know that the church is still ministering and that a new era has begun. Be sure that nothing negative ever appears in your printed materials, especially the church bulletin. Other people read church publications and some of them like to talk about what they read. Don't give the Enemy any ammunition.

Bringing spiritual health to a sick church body is a great challenge, but what a joy it is when the health returns and the body starts to grow! It takes love, patience, prayer, and a solid ministry of the Word. Settle it in your mind that you will stay with it until the job is done. If the church changes pastors too soon, it might bring total defeat. "If God is for us, who can be against us?" (Rom. 8:31).

I GREW UP IN THE CITY, BUT I WILL BE PASTORING IN A SMALL RURAL CHURCH. WHAT SHOULD I KNOW SO I WILL DO A GOOD JOB?

First, don't minimize the importance of the rural ministry. Our villages and small towns make up one of the greatest mission fields in the world today. If it's right for a missionary to seek out scattered small villages in some primitive area, why is it wrong for a pastor to minister in a small town in the United States or Canada? In God's sight, there are no small churches—and there are no big preachers.

Generally speaking, the rural lifestyle is different from that in the big city, although city ways are entering into country life. The people of the soil are generally more relaxed, more patient, and more serious than people in cities. They take time to get to know each other. They look beneath the surface. For the most part, they accept the pastor who is sincere and loving regardless of where he grew up.

Rural churches resist pressure and high-powered promotion. You will want to study people's habits and try to enter into their thinking, but you would do this in any church situation. Don't try to make the rural program conform to that of the city. People in small towns live close to the soil and the seasons, and you will want to do the same thing. What the church does must fit into the daily work schedule of the members and not the ideas of the pastor.

People sometimes live miles from each other, and when they come to church, they want to have time to visit. Your own visitation must take these distances into consideration.

While in the city you can make brief visits in apartments; in the country, your people will want you to stay a while and chat. And they probably will want your spouse to visit with you as much as possible. You'll be invited to share meals with them, during which you can learn a lot and do some effective pastoral work.

Ministering in the small community has advantages and disadvantages. Sometimes one or two families (usually intermarried) will get control of a church and the pastor must deal with power blocs. But that can happen in any church. Everybody knows everybody else's business, and the past is not easily forgotten. A small town has been defined as "a place where there isn't much to see but there's sure a lot to hear." Traditions are held tenaciously, but this also happens in city churches. The beginning pastor, however, will usually discover a nucleus of godly people who will love him, encourage him, and make him glad he tarried with them.

Get acquainted with the funeral and marriage customs early in your ministry. Learn by talking with and listening to the old-timers in the area. Be genuinely interested, and your own life will be enriched.

Give the people the best that you have; feed them the finest of the wheat. Never judge your ministry by the number of people who show up, although you do want the work to grow. The potential in many rural areas is not always great, but this should not encourage you to do less than your best. Especially get to know the children and young people—and even the names of the dogs! Many of the young people may move into the cities when they get older, so minister to them while you have opportunity. Those who marry and stay should be worked into the local church ministry. Those who move away should be encouraged to get into good churches in the cities.

Never give the impression that you are ministering only until something better comes along. Be devoted to your people, and if God does open another door, you will be ready to enter it. In the years to come you will be grateful for the opportunity he gave you to establish your spiritual roots in a rural area.

One source of encouragement and helpful materials is the Rural Home Missionary Association (RHMA). Contact them at Box 300, Morton, IL 61550 or visit the organization's Web page at www.rhma.org.

NOTES

REFLECTIONS

ACTION POINTS

Chapter FOUR

Church Organization

*Is there any divinely mandated pattern of
church organization?*

Any honest student of church history must confess that God has
used and blessed people in almost every form of church government:
congregational, Presbyterian, Episcopal, Plymouth Brethren, Quaker.
Reorganizing your church is not a guarantee that God will send revival.

Acts 6:1–7 indicates that the early church was congregational in
organization, but that it respected the oversight of the spiritual leaders.
First Timothy 3 indicates that the officers in the church were bishops
(overseers) and deacons. A comparison of Acts 20:17 and 28 suggests
that the terms *bishop* and *elder* are synonymous and are equivalent to
"pastor." Some churches have the pastor as the leader of the church,
the elders as spiritual leaders with him, and the deacons as officers who
manage the financial and physical operation of the ministry. If the
church is incorporated, the law usually requires trustees.

Regardless of what officers you elect and what you call them, the
church must have leadership. However, church organization must not
become a substitute for the work of the Spirit in the church. A. W.
Tozer said, "If God were to take the Holy Spirit out of the world, most
of what the church is doing would go right on and nobody would know

the difference." A sobering thought. Organization should be a blessing, not a burden, and a means of getting work done, not hindering it. The size of the congregation determines the amount of organization the church needs.

Accept the organization as you find it. If the Lord convinces you of areas that are not scriptural, discuss the matter with your key leaders and give them time to pray and reflect. But don't get the idea that a certain kind of organization automatically wins the blessing of God. God blesses men, not machinery.

HOW DO I FIND AND TRAIN LEADERS IN THE CHURCH?

Preach the Word faithfully, because the Word feeds and equips the saints to do the work of the ministry (2 Tim. 3:16, 17; Eph. 4:11–12). The Word also sifts the people. Back up your messages with prayer, and pray for your people by name. Jesus commanded us to pray for laborers (Luke 10:2).

It is usually unwise to advertise for workers. Often the cranks show up, and then you have to find something for them to do. Quietly watch the congregation and God will give you direction. If you think members have potential, try them out in smaller places (Matt. 25:21) and let them prove themselves. Take people visiting with you and see how they minister in homes. (This is also the best way to train soul winners.)

When you do challenge people to fill an office, tell them the task will be demanding and will require spiritual discipline. Capable people respond to challenges no matter how difficult those challenges may be. Lesser people enjoy merely filling an office and acting important.

Many churches have effectively used "spiritual gift" surveys and "job inventory" sheets that list opportunities for service. (Remember, there are many spiritual gifts other than teaching and preaching.) Each new member ought to receive a copy of the inventory, and it wouldn't hurt to survey the entire membership annually. Leadership training courses and teacher training courses are available from several evangelical publishers, so check with your denomination or your local Christian bookseller.

Carefully select people from the church and disciple them (2 Tim. 2:2), and they in turn can help you train others. This plan takes time, but it finally multiplies the leaders in the church. Be prepared to see several of these leaders called into Christian service and rejoice that your ministry will be multiplied that much more.

How do we remove unproductive officers and leaders?

This is one area that demands a great deal of prayer and patience. Many churches lack dedicated leaders and removing willing workers, even if they are incompetent, seems like suicide. But keep in mind that we reproduce after our kind. One poor teacher can manufacture in his class a dozen difficult church members or equally unqualified teachers. What can we do?

First, always aim for excellence in your ministry and challenge your workers to aim for excellence. Create an atmosphere of excellence and before long some of the incompetents will feel uncomfortable.

Second, make it easy for people to resign or to change ministries. Many churches find it helpful to survey their appointed leadership staff once a year to see if any of the members want to take a year's furlough or move to a different department. It is amazing what happens to a teacher when she is liberated from twenty-one years of confinement in the nursery! Better to unite a couple of classes and give them a teacher who enjoys the work and does it well, than to make one class suffer with a malcontent.

Begin a program of in-service training, with assistant teachers in each department. The assistants should be given opportunity to teach regularly, and the teacher should help train them. Often a poor teacher will sense he is out of place and will want to give the class to the assistant. Be sure that such transitions are without competition or embarrassment.

When you feel your own leadership is secure, suggest definite standards for teachers and officers. You will want to beware of setting up a pharisaical code, of course; but there is nothing wrong with a set of biblical standards for those who lead the church's ministry. A leadership training class or a teacher's training class is also valuable, especially if your code requires all future leaders to graduate from the course.

Try to place your new converts and new members on committees or in classrooms just as soon as they are ready. The usual problem is the unwillingness of some of the older members to relinquish their places. In some cases, a resignation (or a funeral) seems to be the only answer, although we don't think it's wise to pray for funerals. Take it to the Lord in prayer and let him handle each case in his way and in his time.

Be sure you know your leaders personally before you start using surgery. The better you understand their lives and homes, the better you will know why they seem to be misfits, and where they can fit the best. Above all, don't try to remove leaders simply because they don't agree with you. Find out why they disagree; they may have some legitimate insights that you have missed. Of course, a persistent troublemaker must be dealt with (Titus 3:10–11).

Is there a biblical plan for church finances, and to what degree should the pastor be involved?

The biblical plan seems to be the bringing of tithes and offerings to the Lord by the believers in the local assemblies. First Corithians 16:1–3 deals with a special offering for the poor, but the principles are the same. Second Corinthians 8–9 is a great passage to study on the matter of church finances. You will note that the giving was church-centered (8:1), from the heart (8:2–9), proportionate (8:10–15), and handled honestly (8:16–24). The right kind of giving brings blessing to others (9:1–5), blessing to the giver (9:6–11), and glory to God (9:12–15). The emphasis in these chapters is on the grace of giving (8:1, 6–7, 9, 19; 9:8).

If the sheep are properly fed, they may be milked and shorn. Some pastors forget that the biblical shepherd kept his sheep for their wool and milk and for reproducing—not especially for their meat. For a pastor constantly to be butchering the sheep is tragic for the church. When God's people receive a balanced diet of spiritual food and willing service, they're only too glad to give. One word of caution: the pastor must not try to find out how much each member gives. Those records must be kept confidential and the pastor is better off not knowing what the records say.

It's our conviction that people should be taught to give to their local church and through their local church. It is unfortunate that there is so much competition for the evangelical dollar these days. If every believer were faithfully giving to his own local church, there would be "bread enough and to spare" for the local ministry and for sharing with other ministries. No pastor can force his people into any pattern of giving, nor should he want to. But it's unfortunate when church members send God's money all over the world and yet fail to support their own church. Oswald Smith said, "The light that shines the farthest will shine the brightest at home." Galatians 6:6 teaches that believers should share material blessings with those who minister to them in spiritual things.

Luke 16:1–12 indicates that there is a definite relationship between how a servant of God handles spiritual things and material things. More than one minister has lost his testimony and ruined his ministry because of the mishandling of funds. This explains why Paul was so careful to have messengers from the churches with him when he carried the gift to the Jerusalem saints (2 Cor. 8:16–24). Budgets, finance committees, and audits may seem to be nuisances, but they are wonderful safeguards against the accusation that the pastor is not honest with church funds. The pastor ought to work closely with his officers in these matters. If the pastor is not concerned about the financial aspects of the church, it is doubtful whether the members will be.

Whatever you do, don't harp about money. The expository preacher who leads his people through the green pastures of the Word will have many opportunities to teach Christian stewardship. Also, don't bring your own personal finances into the pulpit. We heard of one pastor who complained in a sermon that he had to dip into his savings account to buy a new suit. Many of his listeners did not even have a savings account.

Conducting a membership orientation class is a wise thing. It's a good place to share the financial needs of the church and teach new converts and new members the biblical principles of giving. Many churches mail out quarterly or annual statements of giving. A good tract about stewardship could be included. And don't overlook the possibilities of the members naming the church in their wills. Talk to a reputable Christian stewardship expert about setting up a will clinic in your church or making estate information available to your members.

J. Hudson Taylor was right: When God's work is done in God's way, for God's glory, it will never lack God's supply. God is not obligated to pay for our selfish schemes. He is obligated to support his ministry.

Is it right for a church to have a savings account when there are so many needs to be met at home and on the mission fields of the world?

It's not unscriptural to save money or to collect interest. In fact, Christ's parable of the talents is built on that theme. Nor is it wrong for a church to plan for the future, provided the church doesn't turn into a building-and-loan association and become so obsessed with money that it loses its spiritual values (Rev. 3:17). In fact, the church that builds its savings and collects interest will save money by not having to borrow.

As for missionary needs, these should be met as the Lord leads and enables; but nowhere does the Bible tell us to tear down the work at home in order to build it up somewhere else. Many mission boards have savings accounts as they plan for future expansion. The careful use of money is a spiritual ministry (Luke 16:1–12) and God expects us to be good stewards of what he gives to us.

The key issues are motive and purpose. If your motive is right and the purpose is in God's will, then a savings account can be a blessing. Most churches had better keep a fund available, since the blowing up of a boiler or the sudden collapse of the electrical system could slow down the ministry for a time. Better to have an emergency fund on hand than to plead for help when the crisis arises.

Some churches include in their annual budget a set amount to be used for missionary emergencies only. The fund is controlled by the pastor, the board, and the missions committee, so it isn't necessary to call a congregational meeting for approval. If a missionary needs emergency surgery or must return home suddenly, the fund can help without hurting the total budget, and you can act quickly without waiting for congregational approval.

THERE SEEMS TO BE A LEGALISTIC ATMOSPHERE IN OUR CHURCH, WITH AN EMPHASIS ON RULES AND REGULATIONS. I HAVE NOTHING AGAINST BIBLICAL STANDARDS, BUT I'M AFRAID OF A PHARISAICAL SPIRIT THAT COULD DEADEN THE LIFE OF THE CHURCH. WHAT SHOULD I DO?

Gilbert K. Chesterton said, "Never take down a fence until you know why it was put up." Often a church becomes legalistic in order to protect its ministry. Instead of trusting the Word, prayer, and the Spirit, church boards sometimes pass restrictive rules and turn pastors into policemen. In time, the rules are considered sacred, even though the situations that called them forth disappeared long ago. We recall a church that established a movie committee because of a staff member who showed a movie they thought was improper. It was basically a censorship board that eventually had no work to do. There is certainly nothing wrong with a church setting up biblical standards, so long as members realize that standards will not change anybody and that not everyone who obeys the standards is necessarily spiritual in his heart.

The danger of the legalistic spirit is that it is based on fear and generates criticism, and a critical church easily becomes a divided church. It also produces spiritual pride and an attitude that "We are better than other churches."

We reproduce after our kind. A critical pastor gradually produces a church full of critical people—and they will criticize the pastor the most. A loving pastor will eventually create an atmosphere of love and acceptance. It isn't necessary to fight the rules; just quietly go about your business and love the people, and the rules will gently sink into oblivion. This doesn't mean you lower the standards of the church. It means you raise the standards by giving the members a higher spiritual motive. Paul had some of this in mind when he wrote Romans 7:14–8:13.

There are three levels of obedience: fear, reward, and love. The lowest is fear—obeying because we have to. The next level is reward—obeying because we get something out of it. The highest level is love—obeying the Lord because we love Christ and our fellow Christians. People don't become spiritual simply by constraint from the outside; vibrant spirituality must come from compassion on the inside. In 2 Corinthians 3, Paul contrasts the legalistic ministry of the Old Testament and the Spirit's ministry under the New Covenant. Every pastor ought to read and master A. T. Robertson's masterful exposition of this passage, *The Glory of the Ministry* (Grand Rapids, Mich,: Baker, 1967). As the people of God mature in the Lord, they have less and less need for rules and regulations and start walking in the Spirit and the love of God.

Nothing breaks the shackles of tradition like evangelism. Start to win souls, and the new babes in Christ will help create an exciting new atmosphere in the church. To be sure, the scribes and the Pharisees will sit on the sidelines and criticize, defending their rules; but love them anyway, pray for them, and keep working.

Chapter FIVE

Preaching

*Is preaching really important to the
ministry of the church?*

Preaching is one of many ways God spreads his Word, but we
sincerely believe it's the most important way. He proclaims his Word at
the Lord's Table and in baptism, as well as in the good works of
individual believers ("Let your light so shine …"). But nothing can take
the place of the Spirit-empowered preaching of the Word of God in
what we know as the sermon. When God would present his Son to the
world, he sent a preacher named John the Baptist to prepare the way.
Much of the Bible is made up of messages delivered by servants of God.
Whether we like it or not, the spiritual level of the church rises or falls
with the preaching of the Word. Church members will tolerate
weaknesses in a pastor, but if the pastor doesn't feed them and teach
them, they will be unhappy. The pastor who doesn't believe in the
importance of preaching, and who doesn't work at being a better
preacher, is going to have a rough time. (Perhaps such pastors should
serve as assistants and develop the gifts God has given them.)

How many politicians or educators could get crowds to come and
hear them week after week, year after year? Yet millions of people
each week go to church to hear ministers preach the Word of God.

G. Campbell Morgan called preaching "the supreme work of the Christian ministry." It is also the hardest work in the ministry if it's done faithfully.

While it takes more than a strong pulpit to build a strong church, the emphasis on preaching must be maintained. Some churches have been too easily influenced by the latest secular fads—counseling, group dynamics, dialogue, drama, and so forth. These have a place in the ministry of a church, but none of them can adequately substitute for the systematic preaching and teaching of God's Word. People may be moved in one way or another by movies and drama, music and debate, but they will never be changed and lifted higher apart from the proclamation of the Word of God.

Perhaps the main reason people have criticized preaching is the fact that it is too often poorly done and fails to meet their needs. Pastors who run around town all week, or who travel frequently to seminars and conferences, might think that all this activity is ministry, but it may not be—especially if they manufacture shallow sermons at the last minute. These people are digging their own graves and they may take their churches in with them. Real preaching is hard work. Perhaps this may explain why some pastors look for substitute ministries.

If preaching is important to you as a pastor, everybody will know it. Your congregation will know that you spend time daily studying the Word. They will see you visiting and counseling so that you are better acquainted with the needs of your people. They will sense that you are living by priorities. Most of all, when they hear you preach, their hearts will be helped and they will give thanks to the Lord that they have a pastor who loves them enough to work hard at preaching.

The next time you are tempted to question the centrality of preaching in your ministry, remember what the preaching of the Word accomplished in Martin Luther's Europe and John Wesley's England. Think of George Whitefield and Jonathan Edwards, Billy Sunday and D. L. Moody. And think of your hungry sheep who come week by week to be fed. Paul puts it pointedly: "Woe is unto me, if I preach not the gospel!" (1 Cor. 9:16 KJV).

How can I improve my preaching?

We improve our preaching (and every other ministry we do) by improving ourselves and our walk with the Lord. Begin by never being satisfied with your preaching, and don't believe all the complimentary things people say about it. While we appreciate the encouragement that comes when a message helps a needy heart, we must never become complacent. After he had been in the ministry over a quarter of a century and was preaching to thousands, Charles H. Spurgeon told his congregation, "I am still learning how to preach." The satisfied preacher will never grow. He will become the center of a mutual-admiration society, not a source of spiritual power.

We improve the preaching by improving the preacher. Phillips Brooks was right: preaching is "the communication of divine truth through human personality" (*Lectures on Preaching* [New York: Dutton, 1877], 5). God sends people, not angels, to declare the Gospel. "There came a man who was sent from God; his name was John" (John 1:6). As we grow in grace and knowledge and cultivate a satisfying devotional life, we can't help but improve our studies as well as our sermon preparation and delivery. Better Christians become better preachers and preach better sermons.

Don't be afraid of kindly criticism. In the early days of his ministry, Spurgeon received a card every week from an anonymous hearer, in which the man lovingly pointed out the preacher's errors on the previous day. Instead of resenting this constructive criticism, Spurgeon welcomed it and profited from it. (Here's where taped messages are helpful—if you can bear to listen to yourself preach. A faithful wife is also a helpful critic.)

Hear other preachers as opportunities come your way, not only the well-known pulpiteers but also local ministers who as yet have no fame. You can learn from everyone you hear, either what to do or what not to do. Many excellent preachers have taped sermons available and you can also hear some of them on radio or television. (Warning: Don't become the blind disciple of some great preacher. Thou shalt not worship the tape recorder—or imitate what you hear.)

Read good books on preaching and also read published sermons, even if you don't totally agree with the preacher's ideas. George Morrison used to read a sermon a day, selecting them from many different preachers. Read sermons for your own spiritual benefit first, then read them to gain an understanding of the preacher's technique. Don't imitate but do learn. John Henry Jowett confessed that he often asked himself as he prepared a message, "How would Spurgeon deal with this text? How would Alexander Whyte lay hold of it?" He called this "looking at the theme through many widows" (*The Preacher: His Life and Work* [Garden City, N.Y.: Doran, 1912], 127–28). Index all the sermons in your library so you can locate them quickly by text, and take time to read them and compare them.

Beware of promoting homiletical hobbies. Too many of us enjoy preaching on our favorite themes, and we resist breaking new ground. Paul admonished Timothy to give himself wholly to the ministry and to meditate on the Word "that everyone may see your progress" (1 Tim. 4:15). The word translated "progress" means "pioneer advance." Paul wanted Timothy to be a pioneer, moving into new territory in the Word and finding fresh truths to share.

There's a wealth of enriching spiritual food in the proper use of the original languages of the Bible. We say "the proper use" because there's a wrong way to use Hebrew and Greek. Your people want the meal, not the recipe; and pelting them with "cognates" and grammatical rules can take away their appetite for deeper spiritual things. Leave the academics in the study and take the results into the pulpit. There are many excellent linguistic tools available today, even for the minister who hasn't been trained in biblical languages. Learn how to use them and you can't help but grow and help your people grow.

If you're sincere in wanting to improve your preaching, God will give you opportunities to do so. He will permit situations to come to your life that will drive you to the Word and prayer. One of the best places to go deeper into God's Word is in the furnace of affliction. When God wants to proclaim a message, he prepares a preacher. Be that preacher!

CAN YOU GIVE ME SOME SUGGESTIONS
FOR EFFECTIVE SERMON PREPARATION?

Be yourself, your best self, of course, but yourself—a voice and not an echo. Many of us prefer expository preaching, and we heartily recommend it to you. But many effective preachers were not expositors of the Word: Phillips Brooks and George W. Truett are two classic examples. Please don't imitate some great preacher and miss the ministry God has planned for you.

Plan your preaching. Don't spend most of the week frantically hunting for something to say. Preach through a book, or give a series of messages on a connected theme: the prayers in the Bible, the parables, the miracles, or character studies. It is amazing how the Spirit uses messages in a series to meet needs that we didn't know even existed. Don't become a slave to a plan, however. If some crucial event occurs, or if God burdens you to give a different message, by all means follow the Spirit's leading. In fact, interrupting a series will make the message that much more significant. If you know where you are going week by week, you can be thinking ahead and dropping ideas into your sermon file folders.

Start working early. If you are preaching through a book you can do your spadework on a larger section than you intend to preach from, and in that way get ahead for the subsequent weeks. Start early in the week and early in the day. Give yourself some deadlines and try to have Sunday's message in final form by Friday noon. Nothing is more frustrating than trying to get a week's work done on Saturday afternoon.

Be systematic. Many preachers use a desk portfolio to keep their notes in as they study. You can find these portfolios in your local office supply store. Have one page and pocket set aside for each message or speaking assignment. Take your study notes on pieces of paper, perhaps three inches by four inches, instead of on large sheets. (We suggest you save all paper that has a clean side and get a printer to cut it for you.) Put only one idea or fact on each little sheet. When the time comes to organize your notes, all you have to do is sort out the papers.

Start with the Word of God. Before you turn to your books, concentrate on God's Book. First, find the main message of the passage and then jot down the ideas the Spirit gives you as you meditate and pray for light. Consult the original languages and use several translations. After you've done your own original spadework, then turn to the commentaries and correct any wrong ideas you may have had. Ask yourself these questions about the passage: What does it say? What did it mean to those who first heard or read it? What does it mean to the church today? What does it mean to me personally? How can I make it meaningful to others? Don't bypass the last two questions. A sermon becomes a message only when it is filtered through the heart and the life of the preacher. Phillips Brooks told ministerial students to find the place where divine truth touches human life, because that's where your message is.

Organize your material. Clear preaching begins with clear thinking. You should be able to state the thrust of your message in one concise sentence. "The church that prays will experience the blessings of God" tells the people what the theme is and how you plan to develop it. Your main points should explain and support this "sermon sentence" or proposition. An outline is important because it helps you digest your message so you can preach with freedom, and it helps the people follow your message and remember it. However, don't let the outline become so obvious or clever that it distracts from the message.

Let the Lord use you. Sermon preparation is a spiritual experience. It can be compared with wrestling, or fighting a battle, or even the travail of a woman with child. The Spirit must speak *to* us before he can speak *through* us, so receive God's message in your own heart and ask, "What does this truth mean to me?"

Keep in contact with your people. There is no conflict between pastoring and preaching: they complement each other. As pastors, we get to know the needs of our people; as preachers we use the Word to meet these needs. Often you will find a message springs full-blown in your heart while ministering in a hospital room or standing at an open grave. The ivory-tower preacher who descends twice a week to deliver an oracle and then retreats into his study, may have great scholarship and homiletical excellence, but he will not have the warmth and personal touch that is so necessary to effective preaching. The sermon will be the "sea of glass" but not "mingled with fire." "Within the veil" (spending time with God) and "without the camp" (spending time with God's people) are two phrases from Hebrews that describe the life of the balanced minister.

Keep alert! We're always preparing messages, so keep your eyes and ears open for illustrations, ideas, and new approaches. Jot down the ideas that come to you or you will forget them. Keep an "idea notebook" or file folder and add material to it. Andrew Blackwood called this the "sermonic seed-plot." You never can tell when some seed might blossom into a helpful sermon just when you need it. Each minister must work out his own schedule and approach. The old adage is right: "Plan your work and work your plan." And keep in mind that you're involved in eternal business that deserves the very best you can give.

How can I keep a balance in my ministry so that I don't ride a hobbyhorse and fail to preach "the whole will of God" (Acts 20:27)?

Spurgeon told about two farmers who met at the Monday morning market. "Did you go to church yesterday?" the one asked the other. "Yep," was the reply. "Well, what did you hear?" "Oh, the same old thing—ding-dong, ding-dong, ding-dong!" "You're fortunate," said his friend. "All we ever hear is ding-ding-ding-ding!"

Your personal growth, through study and pastoral service, is the best way to assure your people a balanced diet from the Word. Second Timothy 3:16 commends to us "all Scripture," and Jesus said, "Man does not live on bread alone, but on every word that comes from the mouth of God" (Matt. 4:4). Keep digging into the Word and daring to pioneer into new territory, and you and your people will grow.

This is where expository preaching becomes valuable. The wealth of the Word makes demands on those of us who preach it. You can't play the music of heaven on one string. Let God direct you to a Bible book that excites you and preach your way through that book, come what may. We suggest you select the book carefully, and read it through several times, before announcing a series. Otherwise you may begin to build the tower and find you can't finish it.

Major on the great themes of the Word and avoid clever sermons on obscure texts. Deliberately tackle passages that you have avoided or even feared. Plan your preaching so there is balance. A wise wife plans menus and a wise pastor plans messages: Old Testament and New Testament texts, exhortation and edification, duty and privilege, history and prophecy, conviction and encouragement. Of course, we always preach Christ and the Gospel, no matter what the text.

Just because one preacher can preach for ten years in Romans doesn't mean that every preacher is supposed to do it. Early in his ministry, W. Graham Scroggie began a long series on Romans and saw his congregation dwindle. A note from one of his listeners convinced him that his plan was foolish, and ever after that he stuck to short series. Spurgeon told about a man who preached for years in Hebrews. When he came to Hebrews 13:22—"suffer the word of exhortation" (KJV)—Spurgeon commented, "They suffered!" There are those few gifted souls who can preach through a book, verse by verse and phrase by phrase, and keep the messages interesting, but unless we have those gifts, we had better concentrate on preaching paragraphs that take us through the book in a sensible length of time.

It's vital that the pastor know the spiritual needs of the flock and meet them accordingly. This is why pastoral visitation and personal counseling are important. Variety and vitality are an unbeatable combination for preaching helpful sermons.

SOME PEOPLE IN OUR CHURCH THINK I'M LIBERAL BECAUSE SOMETIMES I QUOTE OR REFER TO OTHER TRANSLATIONS OR PARAPHRASES OF THE BIBLE. MANY OF OUR NEW CONVERTS AND YOUNGER MEMBERS USE A VARIETY OF MODERN TRANSLATIONS. WHAT SHOULD I DO?

Don't criticize or belittle any translation, especially the beloved *King James Version*. Most church members know very little about the factors involved in Bible translation and they use whatever version "talks to them" and that they're comfortable with. Feel free to amplify its meanings and explain some of the archaic phrases, but never belittle it.

The local church is the only "school" where the students choose the edition of the textbook they're studying. Many churches find it practical to go through the process of selecting a translation that becomes the "pulpit and pew Bible." During the process, you'll have opportunity to explain how the Bible came to us, why there are various translations, what difficulties translators have in doing their work (perhaps a missionary can help you here), and how whatever translation the congregation selects must be able to "speak" to all ages and people on many different spiritual levels.

Every translation has its strengths and weaknesses, and you accept a translation for its strengths and in spite of its weaknesses. If you are acquainted with the languages of the Bible, you can be fairly independent of translations in your own studies. For most Christians, it is simply a matter of education, and this takes time. (We knew a dedicated church member who actually believed the Bible was written in Swedish!) It is necessary to warn your people against popular translations that may not be accurate, but do so with kindness. Some translations and versions we use for leisure reading, and others we use for close study. Some are excellent for their treatment of Greek tenses, others for their scholarly notes. Some churches have conducted a Bible study fair, with the young people manning booths that display various translations and aids to Bible study. The young people explain to the visitors the merits of the translations and the uses of the aids.

If the majority of your people use the *King James Version*, then use it yourself. If you sense there is need for a change, then work with your officers and plan the change carefully. Often adult Sunday school classes are easier to influence than the entire church; but be careful not to split the church while trying to unite them in the Scriptures. And be sure that the version you adopt is really an improvement.

Don't allow your people to make Bible versions a test of fellowship or spirituality. There are a few fussbudgets in almost every church who think the version they use is God's only Word to us. Love them, be patient with them, and be thankful they read the Bible at all. Better that these problems be handled in personal conversation than in public meetings.

Chapter SIX

The Pastor and His Books

I'm not "the student type." Is reading that important?

If by "the student type" you mean somebody who isolates himself or herself in an academic ivory tower and does nothing but study, then we're glad you don't qualify. That kind of pastor is usually academic and unapproachable, or as one church member said, "Invisible during the week and incomprehensible on Sunday." Reading is important in every calling, and the old slogan is still true that "readers are leaders." As ministers, we must "take in" before we can "give out." If Charles Spurgeon were to preach in your area, or if John Calvin were to lecture, you'd go to listen; but their books are available for you to read at any time. Let's take advantage of the vast treasury of knowledge that's available to us today.

We read for *enlightenment* on the Word of God, people, ourselves and our work, and the world around us. The more light we have, the better we can live the Christian life and help others live it. We also read for *enablement*—the "how to" books—and learn how to be better speakers, counselors, leaders and spouses and parents. But we must not stop there, for we also read for *enrichment*, for the growth of the mind and the soul. Here's where the great classics come in, the books that have enriched people for centuries. If we read only the "books of the hour"—the so-called "best sellers"—then we'll never have time to read the books of the ages. Some of these books should be read over and over because there's so much in them that's contemporary and that doesn't have to be rewritten. We read professional books in order to do a good job making a living, but we read other books in order to make a life, and both are important. You'll be amazed at how your knowledge of the Bible will help you better understand and appreciate the great literature of the past.

We want to add this: we also read for *enjoyment*. To enjoy a good book is a treat for an active mind. We usually read to *stretch* our minds, but sometimes we need to read to *rest* our minds and get away from the demands of life. Is this wasting our time? No more than when we take a nap or a day off. If all you did was read detective novels or Westerns, your mind would atrophy; but after a demanding day, turning to something lighter helps to relax the mind and prepare you for a restful night of sleep.

Yes, reading is important, and you don't have to be "the student type" (whatever that is!) to benefit from good books, new and old. Consult the best professional books for your sermon preparation, but also read the best books for personal growth and development. Take a book with you to the barbershop or the doctor's office and put that waiting time to good use.

Many excellent books, including entire sets of commentaries, are now available on CD-ROM, so space really isn't much of a problem. You can carry your library with you!

WHAT'S THE BEST WAY TO ORGANIZE MY LIBRARY?

The Dewey decimal system is standard and probably the best, but it can be very time-consuming. You almost need a full-time secretary to maintain it. Most pastors arrange their Bible study books in the biblical order: Old Testament introductions and surveys; Genesis through Malachi; intertestamental period; New Testament introductions and surveys; Matthew through Revelation. You can set aside special places for theology books, dictionaries and lexicons, biographical books, and sermons. It's usually best to keep commentary sets together in a separate place. Regardless of what approach you take, have a system and follow it.

Keep the books you use most often close to your desk or on your desk: a Bible dictionary, an English dictionary, a Greek lexicon, a Hebrew lexicon, concordances (although your main concordance may be happier open on a dictionary stand), and whatever other literary tools help you in your studies. Keep a shelf near your desk to hold books relating to your current preaching plan. For example, if you're preaching through the Gospel of Mark, place all the commentaries on Mark on this shelf. It's also wise to keep the standard commentaries you use frequently close at hand. This saves a lot of up-and-down motion, although the exercise might do us good!

Be sure to index your library; otherwise, you will forget what material you have available. You need not index the commentaries, because they're all in order on your shelves. But you will want to index printed sermons, special studies in miscellaneous books (the parables, miracles, names of Christ, etc.) and material in dictionaries and encyclopedias that you might forget are there. Several standard filing systems are available, including computer versions, so look for the one that works best for you.

You will probably want to file clippings and articles in manila folders. These, too, can be included in your topical filing system. Many pastors record illustrations on three-by-five cards and file them under key themes: redemption, giving, inspiration, etc. Be sure you write out all the necessary information so the illustration is clear and accurate. Nothing is more distressing than taking out an illustration card that reads "boy with dog in lake." Now, what was that all about?

Don't become a slave to a system. Keep your method simple and it will save you time. Don't feel that you must file every clipping, and do clean out the file regularly.

It's vital that your filing system include an index of sermon material in your library. Most sermon sets are indexed, such as G. Campbell Morgan's *Westminster Pulpit* (Westwood, N.J.: Revell, 1954) and Spurgeon's *Metropolitan Tabernacle Pulpit* (Pasadena, Texas.: Pilgrim Publications). But a master sermon index will enable you to locate any message on a given text or theme quickly. You can use three-by-five cards if you wish, devoting one card to each Bible chapter. You need only list the verse, the volume and page number of the sermon, and it is done.

In one of his excellent books, Wilbur Smith suggests that the pastor index articles in Bible dictionaries and encyclopedias that might be overlooked. The average person might not remember that *The Dictionary of Christ and the Gospels* (New York: Scribner, 1907) has a great article in it on "Preaching Christ" and another on "Children." Your index will remind you.

Add to your index the information about every new book you acquire as soon as possible, and mark on the inside cover "indexed." If you permit books to accumulate without indexing them, you'll end up with a gargantuan task and probably decide the index is too much work and not worth it. In that direction lies ruin.

HOW LARGE SHOULD MY COLLECTION BE?

Quantity is no guarantee of quality. Better that you have two hundred useful books than a thousand that only fill the shelves. The pastor cannot afford merely to be a collector of books; time, money, and space are too precious—and the next move to another pastorate could make a man wish he never owned a book.

You want to build your library with books that are tools and not crutches. A good book helps you study the Bible; it does not do the studying for you. Sermon-help books are like TV dinners—good for an emergency, but not wise for a steady diet. You will need the best translations of the Bible, as well as lexicons and dictionaries to assist you with the original languages. Your commentaries should reflect dedicated scholarship; they should tell you what the text says and what it means. Devotional commentaries are fine for devotional reading, or to give you ideas, but they soon grow thin. It is often by "digging again the old wells" and getting back to forgotten writers that we can improve our own preaching ministry.

The pastor who wishes to build up his library should read reviews and consult the bibliographies available. Wilbur M. Smith has written two excellent ones about the older books: *A Treasury of Books for Bible Study* (Natick, Maine: Wilde, 1960), and *Profitable Bible Study* (1951), reprinted by Baker in 1971. Baker also reprinted his *Chats from a Minister's Library*. Harish D. Merchant has edited *Encounter with Books*, "an annotated bibliography of 1600 books on Christianity, the arts and the humanities." It was published by InterVarsity (1970) and is heartily recommended, mainly because the titles were selected by sixty-seven specialists and not simply one or two avid readers. Beatrice Batson has compiled *A Reader's Guide to Religious Literature* (Chicago: Moody, 1968), which covers the "great religious writings" from the Middle Ages to the twentieth century. The emphasis here is not on Bible study books but rather on great literature that deals with Christian themes, classic literature the pastor ought to read for personal enrichment. An old work, but still helpful, is Spurgeon's *Commenting and Commentaries* (Grand Rapids, Mich.: Kregel, 1954; also available from Pilgrim Publications, Pasadena, Texas). Many of the books Spurgeon recommends are out of print but it is surprising how many of the titles he lists are still available or have been recently reprinted. Even if you don't follow his suggestions, you will enjoy reading his pithy comments.

Some seminaries and Bible schools have bibliographies available, and often the leading Christian periodicals issue helpful bibliographies. Of special value is Cyril J. Barber's *The Minister's Library* (Baker, 1974; updated edition, Moody, 1985). Another helpful bibliography is the *Bible Study Resource Guide* by Joseph D. Allison (revised edition, Nelson, 1984).

Get to know the best authors and you will have an easier time finding the best books. Before you invest in a book sight unseen, examine a friend's copy, or see if it's in a local bookstore. (If you borrow a copy, be sure to return it. Keeping borrowed books is the unpardonable sin of the ministry.) If you watch the book catalogs and keep up with the reviews in the best periodicals, you'll gradually acquire a taste for the better books, and you will know which titles are really worth purchasing. If in doubt, ask a pastoral bibliophile who knows. Over the years you will develop special interests of your own, and will probably become expert in some field—prophecy, Bible biographies, or one special book of the Bible. You may decide to acquire every book you can find on the Lord's Prayer, or the words from the cross, or the life of Peter. Fine, but keep in mind that collecting books is not the same as using books, and it can be an expensive hobby.

Books are like clothes or tools: what fits one person's needs and style may not fit another person's at all. What a friend considers the best book may turn out to be the worst book for you. However, most evangelical pastors would agree on the basic titles that ought to be in the preacher's library. In our own study of the Word, we have found the basic books to be helpful, and most of these are listed in the books cited. However, we would warn the beginning preacher against purchasing a book simply because somebody important or well-known says he ought to. We've occasionally done this, only to discover that we've filled our shelves with useless material while emptying our pockets of needful currency. Now we look before we buy. We suggest that you do the same.

Of course, you will also want books relating to nonbiblical subjects as well, such as history, biography, and general literature, as well as the recognized classics that still speak to us. These will vary with the interests of the pastor. The pastor's learning must always be expanding. The Bible is God's truth, and no book can ever take its place. But the best writings of the best Christians and other scholars will help us in our studies into truth. Never be afraid of truth, for all truth ultimately must come from God. Phillips Brooks often reminded his people that "all truth intersects," since God is the source of all truth. No matter what area of truth we are studying, it must ultimately lead us to Christ who is the fullness of God's wisdom.

BOOKS ARE EXPENSIVE! HOW CAN A PASTOR ON A LIMITED BUDGET PURCHASE THEM?

Some churches now budget an annual book fund for the pastor and the books purchased with this fund belong to the pastor, not to the church. You can enroll in book clubs and other money-saving plans to secure books for your library, and be sure to search the Internet for titles that you need. Watch for bargains listed in publishers' overstock sales, shopworn items, and special sales at conferences. Visit the secondhand stores in your area, the Goodwill Industries, or the Salvation Army. Often you will find excellent volumes at very low prices.

Finally, never buy a book simply because it's priced low. A book you'll never use isn't a bargain; it is a thief.

TIME IS PRECIOUS. APART FROM SERMON PREPARATION, HOW WIDELY MUST I READ?

Wide reading is important to a growing pastor. Everything you read can be used in your ministry. Bishop Quayle observed, "Every department of human thought must be the preacher's concern." We are humans, made in God's image, and servants, called to share his truth, and the more widely we read, the better we can do our work and the easier it will be.

Your own interests and tastes will dictate much of your reading, but you must avoid reading the same kind of book over and over. During your pastoral visitation, stop at the library for a quarter of an hour and browse among the books. Note the special shelves containing new listings. Most libraries issue regular bulletins with their new titles listed, so get on the mailing list. Read book reviews in the better newspapers and magazines, secular and religious.

Along with contemporary books, the pastor should read the

newspaper and a good news magazine. All of them have their faults, so select those that do the most for you. Of course, you will want to read the best in religious journalism, too.

An ideal time to catch up on your magazine and newspaper reading is just before and after meals. A pastor who is privileged to have lunch at home can use part of his lunch period for relaxing reading (providing his family does not have something that needs to be discussed). Ten or fifteen minutes devoted to reading before and after your evening meal will help both mind and body. It is amazing how much reading can be done when you wisely invest short segments of time.

Ask your pastor friends, and the good readers in your church, what they're reading. Often a recommended book becomes just the title you were looking for.

Again, while focusing on the contemporary, don't ignore the great books of the past. Wasn't it Mark Twain who defined a classic as "a book everybody talks about but nobody reads"? There are some books that we ought to read and know simply because they are fixtures in world literature: *Moby-Dick*, *Walden*, *Pilgrim's Progress* (it is amazing how many pastors have never read Bunyan's classic), and others that are recognized as great literature. Many pastors take a classic along on vacation and read it. At first, this reading may be a chore; and then the spell grips them and they say, "Is this what I have been missing all these years?"

A pastor can't afford to be a bookworm but neither can he afford to ignore books. The secret is balance, and it may take you time to discover your own best schedule.

HOW CAN I DISCIPLINE MYSELF TO BE A BETTER STUDENT?

When God calls, God equips and enables. God may not make you another John Calvin or Carl F. H. Henry, but he will help you fulfill your potential. He will give you a love for the Word and a desire to study it and obey it. You need the Word not only for yourself, but also in order to feed your people. A careless ministry is a curse, and the congregation is to be pitied that must listen to a pastor who is unwilling to prepare himself and his messages.

One of the qualifications for the pastor is "able to teach" (1 Tim. 3:2), and this involves "able to learn." The Greek word here is *didaktikos*; it has come into the English language as *didactic*—"fitted to teach, instructive." We must be receivers if we would be transmitters. The pastor can't afford to be like the spider and spin everything out of his own mind; nor can he be like the ant and steal morsels from others. He must be like the bee and gather nectar but "make his own honey." (Bacon used this comparison; we borrowed it from him.) Or, to change the image, pastors milk a lot of cows, but they churn their own butter.

Scholarship is a stewardship; we will answer to God for the use of our time, abilities, education, and opportunities. With God's help, pastors who hate to study Greek can learn to use and enjoy the basic tools of the language and certainly enrich their life and ministry. The more we do a thing, the easier it ought to become. Many pastors used to hate visiting; but the more they visited, the more they enjoyed and appreciated it. So it is with studying: give yourself time to grow and reach your stride. But don't use the excuse, "I'm not the student type." There is no "student type." Paul's words are as true today as when he wrote them: "Do your best to present yourself to God as one approved, a workman who does not need to be ashamed and who correctly handles the word of truth" (2 Tim. 2:15). And while you're in 2 Timothy, take time to read 3:13–17.

To summarize: your own personal needs, the needs of your people, and the wickedness of this evil day all demand that we be the best students possible. The sword of the Spirit is as sharp as ever, but we must perfect our handling of it as we face the battle.

NOTES

REFLECTIONS

ACTION POINTS

Chapter SEVEN

Church Services

How can we avoid sameness and
tameness in our public services?

Let's begin with the reasons God's people assemble regularly: (1) to worship and praise the Lord, (2) to receive instruction and equipping from the Word, (3) to minister to one another and encourage one another, (4) to hear about and pray for the needs of the church family and others, and (5) to witness to the lost. The fact that we assemble weekly is in itself a testimony to the community that we believe Jesus is alive. Where there's life, there's growth, and where there's growth you will find variety and change. If "the Spirit of life" (Rom. 8:2) is permitted to guide and empower us, our meetings shouldn't be lifeless and dull. But for us to imitate the Athenians and constantly look for "some new thing" (Acts 17:21 KJV) will only turn the service into a "production"—religious entertainment—and that's one thing we must avoid. Variety and diversity, yes; novelty, no; unity, always.

So, the essentials for preparing each service are prayer and the leading of the Holy Spirit. Some churches pay close attention to the Christian calendar and celebrate not only Good Friday, Easter Sunday, and Christmas, but also Pentecost, Epiphany, Trinity

Sunday, and other major events that carry spiritual significance. Each service must be an opportunity for worshiping and glorifying God, but we can also focus on missions, evangelism, Christian education, and other themes, and Jesus Christ must always be central (see Rev. 5).

Those who direct the services must be worship leaders seeking to honor the Lord and not cheerleaders directing a religious pep rally. *Preparing and leading corporate worship is one of the most difficult ministries in the local church and amateurs must not be in charge.* It takes time to teach a congregation how to worship. We can't please everybody, nor should we try, but we must seek to be biblical and, as we understand the Word, to please God.

While the elements that comprise a worship service are always the same—music and song, prayer and Scripture, giving, hearing the Word proclaimed—how these elements are put together, who participates, and what we are seeking to accomplish will change from week to week. The word "change" is a threat to some people, usually the older members, but a treat to the younger believers, and we must be wise, loving, and patient. The church is a family, made up of people of all ages and at different stages of spiritual development (see Titus 2), and we must keep the entire family in mind as we plan. Mature believers must help the younger believers to grow in grace (2 Tim. 2:2) and should manifest grace as they do it. Anyone who has raised a family understands what a challenge this can be.

When our regular services become predictable, they usually become routine and then ritualistic, and that takes the heart out of them. Balanced worship services must have continuity or the people won't be able to worship together, but they must also have diversity or the worshipers will be able to participate half-heartedly or half asleep. Sometimes the Lord catches us by surprise as he did the Jerusalem church (Acts 4:31) and Peter in the home of Cornelius (Acts 10:44–48).

However, plan for variety in the singing and keep a record of the songs you use. To use only hymns or gospel songs or contemporary praise choruses will make the services tiresome, and to sing praise choruses over and over again mindlessly can be boring. Whether you sing from a hymnal or from words on a screen, variety and balance are important. It is amazing how few hymns are thoroughly understood by congregations. Martin Luther had his people meet during the week to learn the hymns to be used the following Sunday, and he explained their biblical significance to them.

Beware of routine speeches from the pulpit. The pastor should vary his way of welcoming visitors and giving the announcements. There's no reason a layperson can't relieve him of that task. (Some churches have the faith to eliminate pulpit announcements completely and trust the people to use their bulletins.) Many churches give the announcements before the service begins and also ask the people to sign the attendance registers and pass them down the rows. Every group in the church and every Christian organization in the city wants you to "push" its events, but exercise courage and select the most important.

It's vital that we permit our people to exercise the gifts of the Spirit and not be only spectators at a religious program. Asking godly people to share their testimonies in the services can be a great blessing. It's even better when what they share works into the theme of the message. Occasionally ask church members to read the Scripture lesson (or lessons) of the day, but be sure they prepare. It's unwise to draft somebody to read the Bible in public a few minutes before the service. Perhaps an entire family could prepare during the week and read the lesson (or lessons) for the day.

Whether we like it or not, the morning service usually has a more worshipful atmosphere, the evening service (if there is one) is freer, and the midweek service (if there is one) the most informal of all. We know of no scriptural teaching that demands this, but that seems to be the way churches function. There ought to be spiritual unity and liberty in all the services, but the services should not all be structured in the same way. "Business as usual" could eventually mean "out of business."

THE EVENING SERVICE IS RAPIDLY DISAPPEARING FROM MANY CHURCHES. WHAT'S YOUR READING ON THIS?

According to the biblical record, the first Christians met primarily in the evenings on the first day of the week (John 20:19–29; Acts 20:7). For one thing, the first day wasn't a "day off" and people had to work during the day. Christian slaves would have to get permission to leave the master's house and attend the fellowship, and other believers had to work during the day to make a living. These were primarily "house churches" which also met during the week for prayer and fellowship. The early church didn't make an issue of "days" but encouraged the people to exercise freedom (Rom. 14; Col. 2:16–23).

The evening service used to be devoted primarily to evangelism, and church members were encouraged to bring unconverted people to the service. We recall many exciting Sunday evening meetings in a crowded church during which people were brought to Christ, but times have changed. If a church does have a Sunday evening meeting, it's usually earlier in the evening and the focus is primarily on edifying the saints and not evangelizing the lost. Most of the lost people, as well as many of the saved people (alas!), prefer to stay home on Sunday evenings and watch television or play video games. Also, in some places, it's dangerous to be out at night, and the older people in particular hesitate to leave the safety of home.

Churches that have dropped the evening service aren't necessarily apostate or lukewarm; it's just that they've had to adapt to the current changes going on in society. For one thing, evangelism is happening effectively during the week through the personal witness of believers and the organized visitation of trained soul winners, such as the "Evangelism Explosion" program. Except in large citywide evangelistic crusades and in large churches (especially in the "Bible Belt" in the United States) most "spiritual babies" aren't born in public but in their own living rooms, and then they go to the church to make their public confession of faith. The important thing is that the Gospel gets out and people are saved. This was the practice in the early church (Acts 2:42–47; 4:32–35).

If your people want an evening service and will support it, then structure the service differently from the Sunday morning service. Keep it bright and happy, with enthusiastic singing, the best in music, and preaching that is interesting and inviting. We don't like the term "popular preaching" because it smacks of shallowness and performance, but do deal with texts and themes that touch people where they live. Very few people will attend church on a Sunday evening to learn about the geography of Mount Pisgah or the history of Moab, but they might show up to hear about "The Man Who Should Never Have Been" or "Straight Ahead Lies Yesterday."

Whether the congregation is as large as the Sunday morning crowd is immaterial; do your best in planning, preparation, and prayer, and trust the Lord to bless. Even if you don't meet in the church sanctuary, the Lord will be with you and he can still work. To treat the Sunday evening service like an unwanted distant relative who has leprosy is to ask for failure. To be sure, we must give our best attention to the morning service, but that doesn't give us the right to leave the Sunday evening preparation until late Saturday night or Sunday afternoon.

PLEASE GIVE SOME COUNSEL ABOUT THE MIDWEEK SERVICE.

Like the evening service, the midweek service has gradually been set aside, but this need not cause panic. There's nothing sacred about the church's weekly calendar and we have the privilege of adjusting things from time to time so we can best serve our people and win the lost. Some churches now use that time slot for programs for children and youth (Awana, Pioneer Girls, etc.), choir rehearsals, and elective Bible studies, so the church facilities are being used to good purpose.

Other churches devote one evening a week to "growth group" meetings in homes, and usually more people attend these informal sessions than attended the regular midweek meeting at church, and the people spend time in Bible study and prayer. The growth group ministry has great merit, but you must take care that none of the groups becomes a clique and starts to become divisive. John Wesley borrowed the idea of the Methodist "religious societies" from the Church of England and made it the backbone of Methodism. Large "societies" were divided into "classes" and then "bands," so that the people could minister to one another.

If you have a midweek service, it deserves careful preparation but must not be structured too tightly. Let the people respond to the Word as you teach it. Ask them questions; let them share experiences they've had trusting the Lord. "The wind blows wherever it pleases" (John 3:8), so allow the Spirit to guide in both your preparation and your conduct of the meetings. Many people need a "spiritual oasis" during the week, so make the meeting encouraging and inspirational. Regardless of what service you're planning, beware of trying to manufacture spiritual results. Every church needs to pray, whether you gather together in the sanctuary or in homes as small groups (Acts 2:42–47).

A word of caution: if you feel led to make substantial changes in the church's worship experience, then wait until you've been there long enough to know the people and to gain their confidence. Consult with your leaders and be sure the changes are done in God's time and in God's way. Attracting a group of "turned-on" young people while driving away the older people who built the church is hardly a wise move. The whole church family must work together. Change for the sake of change is novelty; change for the sake of improvement is progress.

The key is your own growing spiritual experience. If you are alive in the Spirit's fullness, it will show in your leading of the public meetings. But please don't try to imitate some pastor you admire. Be yourself, and the Spirit will use you to do the job he has called you to do.

MUST WE ALWAYS GIVE A PUBLIC INVITATION?

Always give the Gospel and make it clear that people must trust Christ if they would be born again. You never know who may be there needing that message. Of course, there are more ways to respond to God's invitation than walking down an aisle; but a public invitation at the close of a meeting is a good opportunity. You need not sing for twenty minutes to give a valid invitation. Any Christian hymn or gospel song can be used for drawing the net. We have more than once preached primarily to believers and closed with a hymn of dedication, only to see unsaved people come to be saved. If you announce a closing hymn, then make it clear that this is an opportunity for decision.

After the singing has ended, point out that interested people may want to see you afterward, and make yourself available. Not every baby is born in public. Often I have seen people come to Christ after the close of the meeting. Also, follow-up visits in the home can prove fruitful. One thing to avoid is saying, "Now, if any of you want spiritual counsel, please talk to one of us." Who are these counselors and where are they? How can they be recognized? Be sure to have a specific place to which people can go for personal help. Very few visitors will stop a stranger and ask for counseling. In some churches, the counselors wear an identifying badge, and this saves confusion and embarrassment.

We need not apologize for giving an invitation, but neither should we use the response (or absence of response) as the test of the success of the service. The harvest is at the end of the age, not at the end of the meeting. A public invitation is not necessarily a test of orthodoxy, but neither is the absence of an invitation (or a resistance to it) a special mark of spirituality. Most worship services close with a hymn, chosen to help us respond to the Word we've heard, and extending God's invitation fits right in (Rev. 22:17). Those of us who minister in city churches never know who is in the meeting or what the needs are. For all we know, some stranger may be present who is thinking of jumping off a bridge. A loving invitation could be used by God to bring that desperate person to Christ.

People resent pressure and intimidation in an invitation to trust Christ. If the Spirit is not drawing the net, better that the invitation close. If the Spirit leads you to continue, then continue, but don't substitute human pressure for divine power as you try to accomplish spiritual work.

HOW CAN WE AVOID THE "SUMMER SLUMP"?

We see no reason why the summer weeks should be a time of relaxing our ministry and telling God we are all going on vacation. To be sure, some of our people will be gone, but others will bring visiting relatives to the services, so there ought to be some kind of balance.

Psychologically, it is bad to talk about expecting a summer slump. If we announce one it's sure to arrive, and it may last longer than the summer. Challenge the people to make the summer months count, and throw yourself into the program with zeal. Tell your people to enjoy their vacations and come home ready for work. In fact, challenge them to witness for Christ while they're on vacation and provide them with the tools. It may take a few summers, but you can actually turn vacation time into harvest time.

Plan a special sermon series for the summer weeks, but not the exposition of a Bible book. People will be in and out of town all summer and will miss too much. Deal with the Psalms, the parables or miracles of the Lord, or practical topics that Paul called "anything that would be helpful to you" (Acts 20:20). If you take a summer vacation, secure the best pulpit supply you can. Start promoting early so the people will know that the church will be in business all summer. In fact, since other churches in your area may retreat during the summer, you can actually reach many new people who are looking for a place to worship.

Make plans during the winter to use your college students when they return home for the summer, and put the teenagers to work as well. Many churches profit from conducting Child Evangelism Fellowship five-day clubs, which are simply miniature vacation Bible school programs held in somebody's back yard for the purpose of reaching neighborhood children. If you live in a city, you can conduct these in various locations all summer long and reach souls for Christ and children for Sunday school. The day camp program is also effective. The children meet at church and are bused each day to facilities for a full program of recreation and Bible lessons. It is somewhat of a mobile VBS. Your local Child Evangelism Fellowship director can give you information and provide tools and training for these special ministries.

We see the summer months as a great time to do special things with children, young people, and college students who are busy during the rest of the year. Make your plans in advance so the church family can put them on their calendar. It is not necessary to plan a circus to attract them, but do aim for variety and vitality. Make use of God's out-of-doors. People often have more time to serve in the summer than in the winter, so plan ways to put them to work. Summer is a great time for outdoor fellowship and witness, and it's also an opportunity for reaching people who hibernate in the winter. Once we decide that nothing can be done, nothing will be done. Approach the summer with a positive attitude of faith and encourage your people to catch the vision.

How can I make the observance of the Lord's Supper a meaningful spiritual experience for the church?

Too often, the Lord's Supper is tacked onto the end of the service, run through hurriedly, and looked upon as an intruder. Such shoddy treatment is inappropriate. Prepare for the Lord's Supper. Arrange the service so that there is plenty of time to observe it. Choose the music carefully. Try to avoid long, needless announcements. (That is a good suggestion for any service!) Bring a message that focuses on Christ and the cross. In the Lord's Supper we remember our Savior, not our sins; so emphasize his love and grace. The attitude of the pastor goes a long way toward creating the right spiritual atmosphere for the Communion service. If you are impatient or upset because your sermon time is shorter, the people will detect it.

Church practices vary as to the time of observing the Lord's Supper and the frequency of observance. It appears that the early church observed the supper whenever the people assembled, and the house churches probably observed it at the close of their main meal. Keep in mind that work schedules sometimes prevent your people from attending on Sunday mornings, so you may want to have an alternate Communion service available at another time. Some churches have arranged to commemorate Christ's death on an off night, with only the church family invited. This is frequently done during Holy Week on Maundy Thursday. An evening devoted completely to the Lord's Supper can be a high and holy experience.

Have you ever thought of having Communion at the beginning of the service rather than at the end? Then you and the congregation won't be worried about time, and you can adjust your message accordingly. Before they partook of the supper, the leaders of the early church used to dismiss visitors and believers who hadn't been baptized, but we don't do that today. The supper "proclaims the Lord's death, 'til he comes," so there is a message to the lost who are present. If you handle the matter carefully and explain the significance of the Lord's Supper to the believers, the visitors will understand and no one need be embarrassed.

Teach your people the meaning of the Lord's Supper. Prepare your own heart, and suggest to your servers that they also prepare their hearts. Meet with them in advance for a season of prayer and consecration. If your hearts are in tune with God and with one another, God will give a blessing.

Chapter EIGHT

Activities and Programs

How can I best minister to the youth of the church?

Start by loving them and not being afraid of them. Some pastors feel intimidated by their young people because they have the idea that every minister must be a youth expert in order to reach them and help them. That philosophy is false. While there are ministers to whom God has given special gifts for working with young people, this doesn't mean that the average pastor must sit on the sidelines. If you're sincere, loving, and real, they'll respect you; and if you listen to them, they will listen to you. Young people are looking for reality, so be a real person, not a counterfeit teenager. Act like a mature adult and they will accept you; imitate them and they may laugh at you.

Learn how to listen. Even when their criticisms are foolish and their ideas are odd, listen to your youth patiently and try to be positive. This doesn't mean you always have to agree with them, but it does mean you disagree in a positive manner, accepting whatever good points you can. Young people feel good just because they've had the opportunity to get something off their mind. An open ear and an open heart will go a long way toward building a solid youth ministry in a church.

Pray for your young people by name. Some churches provide an up-to-date list of their young people for church officers and other leaders to use in their daily prayer time. You will be amazed at what God will do. Pray, too, for the young people away in colleges and universities, and also for those in the armed services, and keep the church family informed of their needs and accomplishments.

Let the teens participate in planning and presenting the church youth program. Have definite goals and guidelines, but let them carry the ball while you and the sponsors coach. Try not to criticize in public; a private chat with a problem teen will accomplish more.

Everything in the youth program must point toward spiritual ends. The local church may have a hard time competing with other programs when it comes to sports and commercial activities, but you can be sure there will be little competition when it comes to spiritual matters. Give your teens a practical knowledge of the Bible. Where else can they get it? Teach them the Christian way to face and solve problems. Help them to understand and accept themselves. The church ought to create an exciting atmosphere in which teens can mature, discover and develop their gifts, and grow into balanced adults physically, socially, intellectually, and spiritually.

Sometimes the pastor must be the youth director until he can train sponsors. If so, don't look upon this as wasted time: you're investing in the people who are the future in the church. When you touch a young person, you touch a whole family. Ask God to give you dedicated people who will identify with the young people and work with them. Don't be impatient; when the right sponsors come along, you'll be glad you waited.

Keep your youth in mind when you prepare for the Lord's Day. It is good to remember them in the pastoral prayer. Be sure there's spiritual food for them in each message. Try to keep in touch with what's going on in the schools, and be sure to give recognition when your teens achieve something special and worthwhile. Sometimes a handwritten note is in order—young people enjoy getting "snail mail" as well as e-mail.

If your high school crowd seems impossible, minister to them the best you can, but start working with the junior high students and grow yourself a group of dedicated teens. It will take two or three years, but it's worth it. Remember, too, that successful youth groups come and go, so don't be discouraged if next year's crop is not as dedicated as this year's. After high school graduation, many of your teen leaders will take off and you will have to start all over, so plan ahead. Be on the lookout for good leadership and keep some "Timothy teens" in training.

Try to plan youth programs well in advance. In fact, there is no reason why one month's programs should not be in the works while the next two months are being planned. Brainstorm with the teens themselves and you will be amazed at their good ideas. Variety is important: change the themes; change the locations; vary the participants; plan some surprises. During the summer, take advantage of the out-of-doors. If you plan your youth calendar, you will have fewer program crises.

Don't be discouraged. Often the most heartbreaking teenager will turn out to be an effective Christian servant or leader in the church. When you're tempted to give up, remember what you were like as a teenager, and get back to work.

Build a growing library of materials that can be used for youth activities, but avoid canned programs that treat teens like kindergarten children. They need resource materials, not prepared speeches.

Finally, teach your young people how to win souls. Witnessing young people are growing young people. You will have fewer problems with teens who are concerned about reaching their friends for Christ. Teens who are excited about Christ will want to share him with others, so give them the opportunities. As a steady stream of new Christians flows into the group, you will have fewer problems with cliques and with finding enough participants for ministries.

Should the pastor teach a Sunday school class?

Some pastors should and some pastors should not.

In favor of the pastor teaching are these considerations: he knows the Word and should be "able to teach"; he can set the right example and show the other teachers how be effective in teaching the Bible; he ought to have a keen interest in the success of the Sunday school, and teaching is one of the best ways to show this interest; he has the time for visitation and the cultivation of a successful class; and teaching a class is a great opportunity for soul winning and making contacts with new families.

Now for the negative: teaching a class can wear him out and make preaching the Sunday morning sermon a bit difficult. When he leaves the church, he leaves a vacancy that might be difficult to fill. Sometimes the new pastor doesn't want to teach a class. Preparing to teach could rob him of time that ought to be spent on other church responsibilities. And other teachers may feel that the caliber of their teaching does not match the caliber of the preacher's teaching.

We think the pastor ought to teach a class if his health permits it. Most likely, he will teach an adult class, so others can profit from his ministry. We reproduce after our kind, and there is no reason why the pastor's class shouldn't be a provider of future teachers in the Sunday school. The argument that other teachers cannot compete with the pastor is childish: nobody in God's church is competing with anybody. We are "God's fellow workers" (2 Cor. 6:1). The pastor's teaching ought to help raise the level of the whole school.

Is there danger that the pastor will use up all his material in a class and thus rob the whole church? Hardly! The Bible is full of spiritual riches, and if a man preached or taught forty times a week instead of four, he could not exhaust it. (He might exhaust himself.) Many pastors have found that the spadework done for a Sunday school class has unearthed treasures they can use in the pulpit. If you are steadily digging into the Word, you will have no problem discovering the spiritual riches you need for each ministry responsibility during the week.

When you arrive on the field, give yourself time to locate the class God wants you to teach. If you take the class the former pastor taught, be sure everyone understands that this is temporary. You may discover a serious weakness in some areas of the school and want to center your ministry there. Build up that area, find somebody to take it over, and then move to another area.

There should be no competition between being pastor and being a Sunday school teacher. Members of the classes might try to create problems ("We want to attend the pastor's class!") but these can be handled personally and with kindness. Some pastors like to teach an auditorium class that is composed of any and all adults who want to attend, including visitors who wander in. This large class becomes a feeder for the other departments. However, it can also become a magnet to draw away people who ought to be in other classes.

As a church increases in size, there's a greater need for small groups, such as Sunday school classes and growth groups. It's here that people get acquainted, discover their gifts, and find their work for the Lord. Use your Sunday school to recruit and train adults, and you will probably reach the whole family. It is here that the pastor can have a very effective ministry.

HOW DO I GO ABOUT ENFORCING AGE LIMITS IN SUNDAY SCHOOL CLASSES AND OTHER AGE-GRADED GROUPS?

With difficulty!

For the most part, children and teenagers are no problem; it's the adult constituency that gives us the most trouble. ("A friend is somebody who remembers your birthday but not your age.") There are two ways to handle the situation, but they may not solve the problem. One is to let a class grow old with the teacher and stay together until it has to be divided. Some Sunday schools reorganize every three or four years. This is sort of a religious "fruit basket upset" but if it is done in the right spirit it can help level the age divisions.

The second suggestion is to organize an open class for adults, somewhat of a catch-all for those who don't want to identify with a graded class. Sometimes the pastor's class, or the auditorium class, falls into this category.

An old backwoods preacher hit the nail on the head when he said,

"Learn to cooperate with the inevitable!" You will have a difficult time trying to enforce strict age limits, and it's our conviction that narrow age divisions are not good for a growing Sunday school. After all, this is a volunteer group and nobody has to come. To regiment adults in the name of religious education might be a dangerous enterprise.

Many Sunday schools have had great success with adult electives. This program permits the adults to group themselves at least once a year on the basis of lesson interest and not age. But no matter how hard you work at it, you will still have some very fine adults whose theme song is "I Shall Not Be Moved." Learn to laugh it off and live with it without erasing the sensible guidelines that every organization needs if it is to prevent chaos.

How can I help improve the music ministry in the church?

Our friend, the late J. Vernon McGee, once said, "When Satan fell, he landed in the choir loft!" One seminary professor called the music ministry "the war department of the church." Alas, in some churches, this is true, but it need not be so.

Let's begin with a basic principle: the music in the church ought to be the expression of the spiritual life of the church. Colossians 3:16 relates music to the ministry of the Word, the mutual edification of the church, and the condition of the believer's heart. In other words, if there's trouble with the music, the heart of the problem is the problem in the heart. The solution is not a new hymnal or an expensive new organ. The solution is a deep working of the Spirit in the hearts of the people. So, in your ministry of the Word, teach your people what it means to sing, just as you teach them what it means to pray.

Good Christians can disagree in their musical likes and dislikes, but spiritually minded people will agree on these propositions: the lyrics must be true to the Word, the tune must be wedded to the words so that one helps the other, and those who present the music must do so from the heart.

With the first, we have no problems: any Bible student can tell when a song is not doctrinally sound. A singer has no more right to sing a lie than a preacher has to preach a lie. It's with the second that we have a real problem, because not every Christian knows when a hymn tune is really suited to the words. Tunes, like salads, appeal to different kinds of people; here we must exercise love and patience.

As to the third proposition, only the Lord (and the musician) knows whether the song is being presented sincerely. The difference between ministry and performance is right here: ministry comes from the heart and seeks to glorify Christ, not the musician. Anyone who ministers in music publicly in a church should obey the biblical truth being presented in the song. Anything less is hypocrisy. To summarize: the music in the church ought to be made up of fit words put to fit tunes, presented by spiritually fit people. Its purpose is to glorify Christ by expressing eternal truth and witnessing to God's greatness.

Congregational singing presents its own special challenges. As the church grows in the Lord, it needs new expressions of its faith and experience. You can't sing "Jesus Loves Me" forever. The choir can lead the way in teaching your people new songs. At first, some of your good people will resist, but present the songs in such a spiritual way that they will be so blessed their resistance will diminish. Tie each song to the Word of God. After the congregation sings a hymn or a gospel song, go over the lyrics line by line and ask the congregation for Bible verses that relate to the words. This can be a thrilling experience for a church and it will make the old hymnal a new book. You might want to preach a series of messages on the old hymns of the faith and the better praise choruses.

There are three keys to good church music: spirituality, balance, and excellence. Avoid music that moves the feet but not the heart. Music that appeals to the flesh can never be used to edify the spirit. Be sure to have variety and balance: too much of a good thing is as destructive as not enough. Keep in mind that your worshipers are at different stages in spiritual growth, and some of the babes have to express their faith, too. Finally, never settle for the mediocre. Aim for excellence. Not every church can afford a gifted music director, but the

Spirit does give gifts to people, and he also brings gifted people to serve in the church. Pray for the kind of music leadership you need, whether a part-time layperson or a full-time minister. And be patient. Don't criticize the music publicly and embarrass people. Work behind the scenes to develop spirituality, balance, and excellence, and God will help you make changes at the right times.

By the way, when others have worked hard to plan and prepare the worship music, be sure to preach a sermon that's worthy of that investment. Don't waste time on trivia. Hit the pulpit running! The music has prepared hearts to hear the Word, so don't go on a detour. If the musicians have done an exceptional piece of work, drop a letter to their leader and thank them.

How do we go about finding dependable missionaries to support?

Usually your denomination or fellowship has missionaries that have been screened and are worthy of prayer and financial support. Avoid missionaries connected with splinter boards, the kind made up of the missionary, his wife, his father-in-law, and his great aunt. You should have a missionary policy that requires all workers to belong to bona fide boards that follow sound business practices such as having their books audited annually, sending out receipts and being led by a qualified board of directors. Many churches require that the boards belong either to IFMA (Interdenominational Foreign Missions Association) or EFMA (Evangelical Foreign Missions Association). If the board is solid, the workers will usually be dependable.

Talk to other pastors. If you're considering a missionary, interview him or her personally and get recommendations from the candidate's home church as well as other supporting churches. Avoid missionaries who change boards or fields repeatedly. Unless they've been interviewed personally and given opportunity to get acquainted with the church and its policies, missionaries should not be put on a church budget.

One area to watch is the recommendations of individual church members. Some of the sheep are gullible and believe everything they read in their third-class mail. Listen kindly to their ideas, but don't commit yourself. Never have a missionary in your pulpit who has not been recommended to you by another pastor or by a missionary whose judgment you trust. The fact that a member of your church is going to the field does not mean the church must give support. It's good to support our own members first, but each candidate must be dealt with individually. This is where a church missions policy is valuable.

Try to have a balanced missionary program, at home and abroad. Some churches send all their money to Africa or Japan and forget that Jesus sent us into all the world. Some churches support evangelistic works only and forget that national Christians also need hospitals and educational institutions. Simply because a missionary family is available doesn't mean we must support them. Keep a total ministry in view, the big picture of a whole world that needs Christ.

My problem is that the church is so missionary-minded that they neglect the home base! What should I do?

Oswald J. Smith said it best: "The light that shines the farthest will shine the brightest at home." We've preached in church buildings that were falling apart because all the money had to go overseas, and the missionaries overseas were using that money to construct and repair their buildings! Acts 1:8 commands us to minister at home (Jerusalem) *while we are also reaching out to other places.* The conjunction is "and," not "then" and not "or." If missionaries lose their home base, what will they do?

Prayer, patience, and preaching; that is the answer. Churches must be educated, and this takes time. Win people to Christ and teach your people to witness, and before long a fire will start to burn at home. Set up a definite financial program for the home base and the missionary ministry, keeping things in balance. Remind your people that it is not a sin to spend money on buildings and supplies at home. Your own missionaries, when they return home, can be a great help. They know that their work on the field is finished when the home churches can't support them.

In your public pastoral prayers, remember your missionaries by name, and try to cover all of them over a period of weeks; but pray for the work at home as well. Give recognition to work done well at home. Don't give your people the idea that God has a special reward for Christians with passports. In time, the attitudes will change, and you will be able to build the home base as well as the missionary ministry.

TO WHAT EXTENT SHOULD THE LOCAL CHURCH BE INVOLVED IN WELFARE OR SOCIAL WORK? IS THIS REALLY A PART OF THE GOSPEL?

The Old Testament prophets thundered against the selfishness of God's people because they failed to care for the needy. Jesus went about doing good (Acts 10:38). The early church helped people in need. We're commanded to "do good to all people, especially to those who belong to the family of believers" (Gal. 6:10). Paul frequently commanded Titus to remind his people to do good works (1:16; 2:7, 11–14; 3:1–8, 14), and by "good works" he meant more than preaching and passing out literature. He was referring to the practical deeds of kindness that help people in their times of need.

The problem is that too many churches substitute good deeds for the witness of the Gospel. It is not a matter of either/or but both/and. Helping men and women with their physical and material needs is in itself a ministry (Heb. 13:16), and it also prepares the way for a further ministry of Gospel witness (Matt. 5:16). We must prove to people that we care before they will believe that God cares. And, if it's right to minister in material ways on the mission field, why is it wrong to do it at home?

Of course, the local church must not abandon the Gospel for social work. But there are people in every church who can visit needy homes, help supply food and clothing, assist men and women in finding jobs, and in a hundred ways share the love of Christ. If Acts 6 is any indication, this work ought to be in the hands of the deacons and their wives (or deaconesses, if your church has them).

It's usually unwise to hand people money out of your fellowship fund. It's better to help them purchase what they need. Many churches keep their fellowship fund supplied by receiving a special offering after the Communion service. Other churches simply vote a designated amount to be distributed by the pastor and the deacons.

Somebody in your church should get acquainted with the welfare agencies in your city. Most agencies are only too happy to cooperate with you and share whatever information they can. It is usually best to check with them before going too far in helping a family. Unfortunately, some needy people go from church to church and rob the saints. We have known of families with several children who farmed out the children into various churches and Sunday schools, especially during the Thanksgiving and Christmas seasons, and in this way reaped a bountiful harvest. The various churches in a given community or neighborhood should keep each other informed about "beggars" who go from one to the other. Our object is to help people, not perpetuate their needs and bad habits. Churches working together can do more for the needy than churches working separately.

While we are on this subject, please educate your church family not to send useless castaway clothing and utensils to missionaries. The philosophy of some Christians seems to be, "It's no good to us, so now it's good enough for the missionaries." We have even been told of church members sending old aluminum foil and used tea bags to the field. Shame on us! Our missionaries deserve the best, not the leftovers.

How can we determine whether the church should go into a building program?

At least four factors are involved: the need, the spiritual condition of the people, the potential resources, and the church's future plans.

If the work is prospering, you will need more space in which to minister. Try to get the maximum use of your space before you start to build. Some churches conduct split Sunday schools that are quite successful. Preaching at two or more morning services is a chore, but it is being done. Some pastors preach at four Sunday morning services! Of course, if the condition of the building is bad, you will have to do something. Watch the growth of the work and keep accurate statistics, not estimates. Before long, you will know if a definite need exists.

To build without discerning the spiritual condition of the people is to court trouble. A building program is difficult enough when the church is spiritual; it would be disastrous with a carnal congregation. It's usually unwise to suddenly spring a program on your people. Start with the leaders of the church. Spend time in prayer and consultation. Try to take the pulse of the church. Are we united? Do we see evidence of spiritual growth as well as numerical growth? Have we the faith to move ahead? Is our faithful stewardship evidence that we trust God and obey the Word? To be sure, you may not reach 100 percent agreement on all these matters but you had better have more than 50 percent. The success or failure of any program involves careful timing, and in no enterprise is it more the case than in a church building program.

Your financial resources are important. Every cloud has a silver lining, but it is sometimes difficult to get it to the bank. Nothing strangles a church like an impossible debt. A sensible debt can be a stimulus to faith and sacrifice, but an impossible debt shackles the church and strangles other important projects. You will always have the doubters who see a depression around the corner, or bankruptcy, or the ruin of the church. These people we love, pray for, and try not to take too seriously. But "in the multitude of counselors there is safety." Evaluate your situation, investigate your resources, and let God give you wisdom and discernment.

Finally, never build without a definite plan for the future. Better to delay building for a year while you draw up a total program than to cripple future expansion because of a hastily built structure. Never build just to impress people, or to relieve a pressing situation. Build because you have a total program for the expansion of the work and because this step is a part of that program.

There are several Christian church building consultants, people of real evangelical faith, who are available to help in these matters. It may cost the church a few extra dollars to secure their services, but the investment could save time, money, and trouble in years to come. It's amazing how many church members who know nothing about engineering suddenly become experts when a building program gets under way. Our Lord's parable about laying a foundation can be applied in more than one way (Luke 14:28–30).

NOTES

_____
_____
_____
_____
_____
_____
_____

REFLECTIONS

_____
_____
_____
_____
_____
_____
_____

ACTION POINTS

_____
_____
_____
_____
_____
_____
_____

Chapter NINE

Visitation

Is pastoral visitation really that important?

If our preaching is to touch and change the lives of our people, we must, like Ezekiel, "sit where they sit" and learn what their real needs are. Hirelings keep their distance and run from problems, but true shepherds follow the example of the Chief Shepherd who always had time for individuals and never kept anybody on hold. Jesus visited homes and shared meals with people and made each visit an opportunity for spiritual ministry. He shared the joys of a village wedding (John 2) and the sorrows of a village funeral (John 11). As busy as he was, Jesus had time to hold the babies (Matt. 19:13–14) and to watch the children at play (Luke 7:31–32).

A high-profile minister once said, "If I walked into a hospital room, I wouldn't know what to say." How tragic to call yourself a pastor and yet not have a shepherd's heart! If you're a younger pastor, you'll discover one day that people will forget your masterful sermons but remember your pastoral kindnesses. Phillips Brooks said that a minister must be a preacher to have authority and a pastor to have sympathy, and he was right—and both are important. No matter what some of the high-profile preachers may do, learn the importance of pastoral care and determine by God's grace to love your people. We can't win souls or shepherd the flock simply by sitting behind a desk or standing behind a pulpit. Read James 1:27 if you have any doubts as to the value of personal visits, and then read Matthew 25:34–46 to be reminded that when you visit Christ's people in their needs, you are really visiting Jesus.

Let's start with pastoral visitation among your own people. Set aside definite times during the week when you will visit the hospitals. Of course, the amount of time needed depends on the size of your community and the number of hospitals involved. Unless patients are very ill, it isn't necessary to visit them daily, and if you have staff assistants or elders with sympathetic hearts, you can share the hospital calling with them. Keep a list of hospital patients in the church office with the necessary information. After each visit, the pastor or elder can add whatever facts he thinks are necessary to help the next visitor. Be sure to mark when the patient has gone home. File the hospital calling sheets for future reference.

New legislation is making it difficult for us to learn when people enter the hospital. Unless the patient gives the hospital permission to release information, the hospital can't contact the church or even give information over the phone. (This may not be true in smaller communities and hospitals.) Therefore, we must teach our people to keep the church informed if they expect to be ministered to and prayed for, especially when there are emergencies.

In smaller churches, the pastor can call in every home in a month or two and then start over again, but whether the church is large or small, we must never make a visit just to be visiting and passing the time of day. We should always have a stated purpose: to get better acquainted with the family; to share some spiritual blessing; or to discuss some vital matter. Be a blessing, but don't waste time. Be spiritually sensitive to the atmosphere in the home. Never give the impression you are in a hurry, even though you may be; and keep in mind that you are laying a foundation for future visits. Visits need not be long to be effective. Do resist the urge to enjoy coffee and cake in every home. Your family and your doctor will appreciate it.

A card file or notebook should suffice to keep a record of the calls made. Arrange your calls geographically whenever possible; it will save you time. When you return home from funerals, plan to visit the deceased's family members who live on the geographical "fringes of the camp."

You should build a list of prospects and unsaved people and keep praying for them and visiting them. There are people in the community, particularly men, who will respond to the witness of a concerned pastor. Some pastors set aside one special time a week just to go "fishing for souls." This is a thrilling experience and really helps stoke the fire for Sunday's preaching!

Don't be discouraged when your visits seem wasted. You're serving God and obeying his Word whether people appreciate the visits or not. It sometimes takes a dozen or more visits before a family will become interested. "At the proper time we will reap a harvest if we do not give up" (Gal. 6:9).

As much as possible, let your Sunday school teachers and church members call on new prospects and people who visit church services. (Most churches use a Sunday registration system for getting the names of visitors. This works much better than the visitors' book in the narthex.) If they feel a contact is encouraging, they can let you know and you can follow through. But remember that, when the pastor visits, he's looked upon as a paid salesman. When members visit a home, they're looked upon as satisfied customers. Visiting, witnessing laypeople who know how to win souls can bring power to a church, so take them with you when you visit and teach them how to do it.

Sunday school calling and religious surveys are programs by themselves. Many churches go once a week to visit prospects and absentees; some go every other week or even once a month. The important thing is to set up a workable program that meets the needs of your church. Simply to imitate another church's program because it's successful may be disastrous.

We say all these things about visitation even though we hear that visitation is an old-fashioned ministry that doesn't work in today's society. Granted, more and more women work outside the home, some husbands have two jobs, and singles are juggling all kinds of activities, and so it's getting more and more difficult to find people at home. But that doesn't mean we should abandon the ministry of personal calling. We may have to adjust our schedules and our approaches, but let's not isolate ourselves from the people we serve.

Some pastors host an evening reception once a month at the church to which they invite Sunday newcomers and people who have been visited during the month. Some of the church leaders should be present, and folks can get acquainted easily as they mingle, munch cookies, and drink coffee, tea or punch. It affords a good opportunity to present the background and ministry of the church. This kind of reception also works on Sundays after the morning worship service.

WHAT SUGGESTIONS DO YOU HAVE
FOR THE PASTOR'S HOSPITAL MINISTRY?

Get to know the hospital personnel and make yourself available to help them, but don't assume authority that you don't possess. By all means get acquainted with the hospital chaplain, even if you are of different faiths. The chaplain has a concern for the welfare of the patients and is glad to assist you.

Visit at hours convenient to the patients. Many pastors find that late morning, after the patients' baths, is a good time to stop by: the patients are fresh and clean, they haven't been worn out by other visitors, and there will be fewer interruptions. Arrange your visits according to the rules of the hospital. Pastors are usually permitted to visit at any time (except in the maternity ward), but don't make a pest of yourself. One pastor we know visited at 11:00 PM and fell asleep praying for the sleeping patient.

Get the facts about the patient. One pastor asked a patient, "Was this an emergency, or did you plan to come in?" The patient replied, "Oh, I planned to come in. I just had a baby!" The hospital was being remodeled so she wasn't in the maternity ward, and the pastor was caught by surprise. A minute at the front desk would have saved him embarrassment.

Be cheerful but not a stand-up comedian. Leave your problems and symptoms outside the door and enter the room determined to be an encouragement. Remain a pastor; don't become an amateur physician. Your seminary degree isn't in medicine. It's wrong to diagnose the case or to compare the patient with others you've visited. Never act as go-between when patients and physicians have a difference. You may not agree with the physician in charge, but you should not declare war. If patients have fears or frustrations, be a counselor and help them find peace in Christ.

Be brief. Unless you are really doing spiritual business and the patient insists that you stay, keep the visit brief. Long visits sometimes do more harm than good. Each visit should help to lift the patient's hope and faith. In most cases, read something brief from the Word and pray to the point. Don't turn the bed into a pulpit and preach to the whole ward. A quiet, personal prayer at the bedside is what the patient needs.

Pay attention to the others in the room; greet them and be friendly. If it's a double room, or three-bed room, be sure to include the other patients in your prayer. If there are other visitors in the room, wait for a break in the conversation and ask, "Would you mind if I prayed for all of us?" Very few patients or visitors would be offended. Often the patients' names are on cards over the beds, so you can mention them by name as you pray. Many pastors have won people to Christ simply by being kind while they visited another patient.

Use Christian literature judiciously. Be sure to read carefully whatever you distribute; the wrong tract can do untold damage. Tell the lost about the Savior. Do it with kindness and love. Better to share the Word when you have the opportunity than to lose a soul while waiting for a better opportunity. It's wise to train your people in the best ways to be a blessing while visiting in the hospital. Often in messages or times of personal fellowship, we have opportunity to warn against deathbed stories, home remedies, loud talking and praying, and other horrible practices that often make Christians unwelcome in the hospital. In fact, some church members should be advised not to do hospital visitation at all. They may not like it, but it is better to upset a few saints than to lose your testimony before the whole hospital.

HOW CAN I ENCOURAGE OUR PEOPLE TO GET INVOLVED IN VISITING AND MINISTERING?

Your example is the most important thing. Visiting is better caught than taught. It spreads best by contagion, not compulsion. Take dedicated believers with you when you visit and ask God to touch their hearts. Once the person has learned the approach and experienced the blessing, they can share it with others. Many Christians have found special joy in sharing in programs like "Evangelism Explosion."

Churches that have a "growth group" program find that the members of the groups care for each other and minister to each other when there are needs. They prepare meals for families with new babies, they help in shopping and special transportation demands, and in many ways surround the person or family with practical Christian love.

At the right time in your ministry, God will burden you to preach on the "going" aspect of the church's ministry. The book of Acts is full of it. Emphasize the *why* and *how* as much as the *what*. Unless the Holy Spirit is in charge, our activities will become more busy work in an already overloaded church program.

Give opportunities for your people to testify of the blessing of visiting, but warn them not to scold the people who don't share in this ministry. Some of your people shouldn't get involved in a calling program, but they can pray for those who do call. Beware lest your busy group of callers become a "spiritual elite" in the church, with a holier-than-thou attitude.

Prepare attractive literature about the church and its ministry so your people will have material to use during the week. Never put negative, critical items in the Sunday bulletin, since this might be used the wrong way. A bright bulletin is a good promotional piece; a sloppy one is better not printed at all.

One more thing: as pastor, be sure that the ministry is worth inviting others to share. The best encouragement you can give your people in this matter of sharing Christ is a ministry of the Word that they can enthusiastically invite people to hear. And keep in mind that, though your members bring in the visitors, it is primarily the pastor's job to keep them coming.

HOW SHOULD WE RECOGNIZE VISITORS IN THE SERVICES AND WHAT'S THE BEST WAY TO FOLLOW UP ON THEIR VISITS?

This depends on the size of your congregation and the location of your facilities. It is a basic rule that no visitor should be embarrassed or put on display. Some people are sensitive and would feel uncomfortable about public recognition. In small churches, the pastor often sees who is visiting because he knows his congregation so well. In larger churches, the pastor can welcome them all—perhaps even have them stand—and they can be given a "welcome gift" to take home.

The guest register in the narthex is often ignored as people come and go. It is better to ask all the people to register each week, using cards or a "friendship folder," and in this way the visitors are not embarrassed by being singled out. Some churches ask visitors to lift their hands, and they then are given a registration card and a packet of materials. The cards are collected during the offering or at the close of the announcements. Friendship books that are passed down each row for people to sign are also available.

The effectiveness of a visitors' recognition time depends on the attitude of the pastor. If he is friendly, he will make the visitors feel at home. If he is reserved, perhaps it would be better if some other member or a couple did the recognizing. Perhaps the deacons could share the ministry.

Some churches have a visitors' reception immediately after the morning service, with light refreshments; and here the pastoral staff and families can meet all the visitors at one time. It's easier to get them to sign the guest book in a reception room, by the way. Each week have different members of the church present to greet visitors and to mix with them.

On Monday morning, either a postcard (prepared exclusively for your church) or a letter should go out to each visitor. Keep the registration card for future use. Perhaps some member of the church could volunteer to serve as director of this follow-up ministry, keeping the records and mailing materials. Once somebody has visited your church, you have the right to return the visit. In most cases, it is better for church members rather than the pastor to return the visit, lest other pastors think he is out to steal their sheep.

During the week, someone from the church should visit the home to thank people for their visit and to determine what the future holds. If the people are active in another evangelical church, simply thank them for visiting. If they are looking for a new church home, or if there are spiritual needs in the home, this fact should be communicated to the pastor.

We believe we owe it to our fellow pastors to let them know if some of their sheep are "visiting around." Sometimes these people are part of problems that you don't want to invite into your church. This doesn't mean that church members have no right to relocate, but such moving should be done in the right spirit. Visitors who criticize their former pastors may criticize you after they join the church, so go easy on trying to build with borrowed bricks.

Chapter TEN

Marriage and Divorce

*How can our church best prepare young
couples for marriage?*

It takes four to get married: a man, a woman, society, and if there's a religious ceremony, God. (Sorry, we don't accept same-sex marriages. See Gen. 2:18–25, Matt. 19:1–9, and Eph. 5:22–33.) A marriage license is required, so that's where society comes in, and the Lord is represented by the presence of the clergy in a house of God.

There are two kinds of preparation: general preparation that's the result of your ministry of the Word and the examples of the married people in the church, and specific preparation as you counsel couples who plan to marry. Every godly couple in the church is an example for engaged couples to follow, and it wouldn't hurt to give some of these veterans opportunity in the services to bear witness of God's grace.

Before agreeing to marry a couple, consider the church and its witness in the community, for what the pastor does always reflects on the church. It's best to counsel and marry people you know, people who are a part of the church family and who will permit you to prepare them for this important step. To marry strangers—especially people "going through town"—is to invite trouble. In many churches, the trustees are in charge of permitting people to use the buildings, and a couple must make a formal application to have their wedding in the church sanctuary. The official board, however, should agree that the pastor may marry privately any couple he believes should get married, but not in the church sanctuary. Sometimes there are emergencies that call for Christian love and not congregational law, matters that have no place on a board agenda or in the record book. We receive our authority to marry people not from the Bible but from the clerk of the circuit court, and, alas, there are times when we perform the wedding as servants of the court.

The preacher who faithfully expounds the Word is bound to cover many themes relating to the Christian home. In Ephesians and Colossians Paul writes to husbands and wives and even to children. Jesus had much to say about family living, and the Old Testament writers deal with the topic, too. Once a year you may want to do a special series on the home, but don't make it too long or too negative.

Be sure that the people who direct your youth ministry give proper place to marriage and the home. The time to prepare husbands and wives is in their maturing years when the material is still pliable. In fact, even the loving care given to little ones in Sunday school is good preparation for marriage.

There should be a selection of books on the Christian home in your church library. You ought to have several copies of the best books available, and make it possible for members to purchase their own copies. Occasional films will also help. Many churches have an annual seminar on the home, with a guest specialist invited to lead the discussions.

Your own home will help prepare couples for marriage, so open it up to the dating crowd and let them see a happy Christian family in action. The way you treat your own spouse and children in public will have an influence on others. When your "marriageables" see you setting the right example, they will be happy to listen to your counsel.

Your specific ministry to a couple should begin as early as possible. When you see that a couple has started dating steadily, let them know you are interested and would be happy to chat with them. God will give you direction here, so wait for his leading; otherwise, the couple may think you're meddling. Set up a series of appointments with engaged couples, and don't fret over the time that it will involve. Better to invest your time helping them build before they are married than to have to invest more time picking up the pieces after the marriage falls apart.

Several publishers have prepared special marriage inventory programs that the pastor can use in his counseling. Many denominations have excellent inexpensive books that can be used as the basis for a series of sessions. It is also wise to suggest that the couple visit their family doctor as soon as possible to talk about the physical aspects of marriage. There are several excellent books available on this subject, written by Christians, and these should be made available to the couple.

Don't assume that, because the couple grew up in the church and have always given evidence of spiritual life, they will automatically have a successful marriage. Just about every church has experienced its heartaches when the "ideal young couple" got a divorce. If you detect any problems (and a good marriage inventory helps here), deal with them honestly and lovingly. If you feel there is need for additional counsel, perhaps from a professional Christian counselor, then suggest that the couple get that counseling as soon as possible. Marriage doesn't *create* problems so much as *reveal* them, and the time to discover and deal with them is before the couple says "I do."

We've ministered long enough to see some marriages that we questioned turn out to be very happy ones, and others that we thought were ideal turn out to be tragedies. It is difficult to make predictions in a matter so intimate as marriage. If you have serious reservations, discuss them with the couple in a frank but tender manner. Pray with them. Encourage them to seek God's guidance and help.

HOW DO WE COUNSEL COUPLES WHO ARE LIVING TOGETHER AND WANT TO GET MARRIED?

If they make no profession of faith in Christ, seek to win them first and then deal with their moral problem. If they profess to be saved, show them from the Scriptures that what they're doing is wrong and must be stopped. Can you hope to prepare them for marriage while they're rebelling against the Lord? If they refuse to stop living together, then refuse to marry them and suggest they go elsewhere. If they agree to separate until they are legally married, then set up a premarital counseling schedule and try to help them understand that what they did was wrong. Divorce statistics are not encouraging for couples who lived together before marriage, so don't lend any encouragement to the practice.

This is an extremely difficult situation to deal with, especially if one of the parties belongs to an influential family in the church or the community. If we act as though nothing is wrong, we'll send out a signal to the young people in the church (who probably know more about the couple than we do) that premarital sex isn't a sin after all. If we lovingly take a stand, it will let people know that you care about your flock and want God's best for them.

You will probably have your share of "crisis weddings," and you must take each one individually. Let your church know that you do not marry people without first counseling them. You may have some opposition here, but ride it out and stick to your position. When emergencies arise, consider the situation carefully and do what God leads you to do. We are dealing with human beings, not checkers on a board. Some marriages that today seem impossible will tomorrow bring joy to your heart. In some cases, your counseling will have to be after the ceremony instead of before; but this is better than no counseling at all.

It is unwise for a pastor to marry strangers. When they phone, let them know you prefer to counsel with people first and that the trustees must give their permission for weddings in the church sanctuary. Not all states list the person's marital status on the license, and you might be performing an unbiblical marriage. It's also unwise and unethical to send these couples to a fellow pastor and put that pastor in an embarrassing position.

DIVORCE AND REMARRIAGE ARE CONTROVERSIAL ISSUES IN MANY CHURCHES. HOW CAN I MAKE THE RIGHT DECISIONS?

Many good and godly Christians disagree on whether divorce and remarriage are scriptural, and the last word probably will not be said this side of heaven. Ask ten pastors for their convictions and you may get ten different answers! The best thing for you to do is to examine the biblical teaching carefully and read widely on every position. Ask the Spirit to guide you, and don't be afraid of whatever truth the Lord reveals. "Each one should be fully convinced in his own mind" (Rom. 14:5). Discuss the matter with wise leaders in the congregation and also with mature pastors you respect. Once you have adopted a position, try to stay with it in love unless your studies reveal some new element.

Beware of developing a holier-than-thou attitude toward people in the church who have had unfortunate marriages. It's possible to be loving and understanding even if you disagree with people.

You will find it best to assess each case on its own merits. We believe that God forgives all manner of sin (Matt. 12:31), and that when God receives justified sinners, we should receive them as well (Rom. 15:7). To preach grace and practice law is inconsistent, and to make divorce and remarriage unpardonable sins is cruel. This doesn't mean that the church should lower its standards and cease to exalt Christian marriage, but it does mean we don't go beyond the Word in dealing with these matters. The pastor who stays in one church for any length of time is surprised almost every year to discover more cases of past marital mix-ups.

If a pastor feels that all divorce is unscriptural or that any remarriage after divorce (for any reason) is unscriptural, and insists that people so involved should not be allowed in the church membership, then he must be consistent by dismissing from the church roll any who violate this position and by refusing to accept into the church family all who violate it. We know of no scriptural precedent for such a position, and we wonder how it could be held in the light of 2 Corinthians 5:17, Ephesians 4:32, and dozens of other verses that clearly teach forgiveness and acceptance in Christ.

Before accepting a call, you owe it to your church to share your convictions in this matter, as well as any changes you make in your views as your ministry progresses. It's our belief that the pastor should have complete freedom when it comes to marrying people, and that he should not be dictated to by a board or a congregation. There are situations that only he and the Lord should know about, and to answer to a board would be to violate confidence. To make views of marriage and divorce a test of fellowship or ministry is, to us, a most unfortunate thing. We "know in part" (1 Cor. 13:12).

Jesus came to "heal the brokenhearted," and that should be our ministry as well. We're going to see more and more marital problems in the days to come, and the answer is not in stricter laws or tougher church membership procedures. The answer is a positive ministry to prepare our young people for maturity and a compassionate understanding for those who have suffered. The church family is made up of all kinds of people (1 Cor. 6:9–11, Gal. 3:28), and the pastor must love and minister to all of them. Love, patience, prayer, the Word, and a practice of Ephesians 4:32 will go a long way toward mending broken hearts and broken homes.

WHAT ABOUT COUPLES WHO "HAVE TO GET MARRIED"?

This problem is more prevalent now and yet doesn't create the same stigma that it did a generation or so ago. Your first responsibility, as we see it, is to help the couple spiritually and minister to the other loved ones involved. As soon as you discover the problem, meet privately with the couple. Seek to lead them into God's forgiveness and acceptance.

Should they marry just because of pregnancy? If they had already planned on marriage and are suited for each other, then they ought to become man and wife. But they shouldn't marry simply because of the pregnancy. They should get married only if this is God's will for their lives. Often the very presence of the problem indicates that they should not get married, that something is radically wrong in their relationship. For them to marry just to give the baby a home, and then eventually divorce, would be adding sin to sin and their marriage vows would be nothing but hypocrisy.

If they don't marry, they must decide on the future of the child. Most communities have agencies for handling these babies, and you ought to help the girl to contact such an agency. She must make the decision, of course, but you can assist her in facing and solving the problems involved. Some girls want to keep the baby as a form of self-punishment, a situation that creates difficulties for the child. In most cases, it is best to arrange to have the baby adopted into a Christian home where it is wanted. Then the girl can make a new beginning in life. Each case is individual, so we dare not make generalizations. The one thing we don't approve of is abortion.

If the couple, or one of the two, is a member of the church, you should guide them into an experience of forgiveness on the part of the fellowship. Again, it's not necessary to display dirty wash, but neither should we make light of sin. It's been our experience that the young people of the church will know about the problem before many of the deacons discover it. If the member is unwilling to make things right, you will have to consider church discipline; but the healing of burdened hearts is the first item on your agenda. Take time, be prayerful, and don't rush to start discipline proceedings. Give God time to work.

If the couple marries, suggest that they have a public dedication of the baby and of their home. This can be done at a morning service, and it will tell the church family and the watching world that the couple is making a new beginning in the Lord.

Sometimes the baby doesn't make it full term or is born with a handicap, and the couple may take this as God's judgment on them and their marriage. You will want to spend time with them and seek to help them through this valley. Don't be judgmental, for only God knows why these things happen (John 9:1–4). Encourage them to let the Lord love them and help them. Keep in touch; sometimes it takes months for these problems to be solved.

SOMETIMES AN OLDER COUPLE MOVES IN TOGETHER TO SAVE MONEY, BUT THEY DON'T WANT TO GET MARRIED AND LOSE FINANCIAL BENEFITS.

Yes, there are old sinners as well as young sinners, but sin is sin regardless of the age of the sinners. Sometimes a scheming senior finds a naïve, willing partner, sets up this arrangement at the partner's expense, and stays long enough to find a more comfortable situation. Paul wrote about people who defended their disobedience by saying, "Let us do evil that good may result." His verdict was, "Their condemnation is deserved" (Rom. 3:8). Paul commanded the local churches to care for godly widows (1 Tim. 5) but he didn't tell them to tolerate ungodly widows and widowers.

Chapter ELEVEN

Death and Funerals

*How can I improve my ministry to the
dying and the grieving?*

Begin by making it the "law of the Medes and the Persians" that nobody will ever joke about death or tell funeral jokes in the public meetings of the church. We have seen some of our people crushed when a guest speaker tried to liven up the service by telling a joke about a funeral. People with broken hearts come to church for comfort and encouragement, not to have their hearts broken again.

The person with a pastor's heart will instinctively do the right thing when the sheep are going through the valley. A dying believer may not know you're at the bedside in the hospital or at home, but the loved ones know, and they'll remember. As a person dies, one of the last senses to go is hearing, so it may be possible to minister to unbelievers and tell them how to be saved. They may not be able to speak, but perhaps they can squeeze your hand to signify they hear, understand, and believe. Yes, we sometimes question "deathbed conversions," but then we remember the thief on the cross.

As soon as you hear of a death in a church family, try to contact the family. Perhaps you should phone first and see if a visit is in order. It's usually best to get to the home as soon as possible, no matter what hour of the day or night. We may set hours for counseling people but not for comforting people. "Be prepared in season and out of season" (2 Tim. 4:2).

Once in the home, try to have a quiet ministry. A talkative, loud pastor is going to do more harm than good. Don't take over the situation. After you arrive, express your sympathy, and stand by to listen and to help. Your visit need not be long. At some time in the visit, offer to read Scripture and pray—and please do this with heart! A perfunctory reading of the Word followed by a routine prayer will only make the wounds hurt more. Ask God to give you compassion.

Try to be at the funeral home before the family arrives for that first viewing. This is the crucial time, and the presence of the servant of God will help the whole family. Walk into the chapel with them, and stand with them silently. Your presence is a sermon; there is no need to preach. Watch for indications of family tensions or problems; see how the people are responding to the death of the loved one and to one another. Half an hour devoted to the family at this point will give you a great deal of insight as you prepare the funeral message and as you minister to the family in later days.

Plan the funeral service to meet the needs of the mourners. The closest relative to the deceased should have the final decision about time, place, and music. Ask whether there is any favorite Scripture that should be read. If you've been in the church a long time, you should already know the family, and your preparation will be simpler. Keep the service brief and to the point; long services often deepen wounds. Your message should focus on one comforting truth; this is no time for a doctrinal exegesis on death or resurrection. You're applying balm to broken hearts, so be tender. People need soothing medicine, not complicated prescriptions.

It's unwise to preach people into either heaven or hell. Yes, we may extol the lives of radiant saints whose confession of Christ was triumphant, but as for others, "The Lord knows those who are his" (2 Tim. 2:19) and it's best to leave it that way. As for those we thought were hardened sinners, we never know what transactions may have taken place between the Lord and that human heart even in the last hour of life. Always give assurance that anyone who trusts Jesus Christ is saved, but that it's unwise to delay that decision.

Try to follow up with a visit in the home as soon as possible after the funeral. Watch for signs of emotional problems. You ought to read widely in the excellent literature available today on the psychology of grief. Be available to the mourners during these difficult days of adjustment. Also, be alert to family disagreements. Bereavement has a way of opening up old wounds or of making people feel guilty. This is one reason why there are often family fights during or after funerals.

Your regular pastoral ministry week after week helps to prepare people for the hour of sorrow. Preach as a dying man to dying people, and when death visits the flock, both you and your people will be prepared.

SHOULD I ACCEPT AN HONORARIUM FOR CONDUCTING A FUNERAL?

Most funeral directors write the honorarium into the total cost of the funeral. Some, however, leave it to the family. It's wrong to ask for one, but if the family involved is not a part of your church they certainly ought to pay you for taking time from your own people to assist them. Since most church members help to pay your salary, accepting a gift from them is another matter. However, you will find that many church members want to show love and appreciation to their pastor in return for his faithful ministry to them. Don't be embarrassed: it takes grace to be a good receiver as well as a good giver. Say, "Thank you. I'll use this in the Lord's work in some way." Many pastors invest funeral honoraria in books, and even write on the flyleaf, "A gift from the _____ family."

There may be times, however, when accepting a gift is unwise, such as when the family is needy, or if the family has served long and faithfully in the church. Suggest that they put the gift into the church ministry as a memorial, or that they share it with a missionary cause. If they insist that you take it, do so, but give it to the church and send them a thank-you note with a receipt. Memorial gifts are being encouraged in more and more churches.

How do I conduct the funeral for a total stranger?

Usually the funeral director calls and makes the arrangements. Get the necessary information from him, including any insights he has that will help you in your ministry. After you have been in a church a few years, you will get to know the local funeral directors, and you will find that they are willing to help you.

Visit the family of the deceased and get to know them. Perhaps there are members in your church who know them, but beware of prejudiced opinions from outsiders. When you arrive at the funeral home, watch for signals that will help you better understand the situation. Your "ministerial radar" will help you here.

Obviously, a funeral message for a stranger can't be as personal as one for someone you know. Deal with the grand truths of the Gospel and the love of Jesus Christ. Don't preach the deceased into heaven or hell; preach to the living and seek to give comfort. Your gracious handling of the funeral service could give you opportunity to minister to the family later and perhaps reach them for Christ and the church.

Should I repeat my funeral messages? How do I develop new messages?

You will no doubt read the same passages from service to service—John 14, Psalm 23, 1 Thessalonians 4:13–18 are everybody's favorites—but you must adapt the text of the message to the needs of the hour. Keep a notebook of your messages, and write on each outline the dates it is used and for whom. Ask God to give you a personal word for each service. To dig out an old message while driving to the funeral home is a sin. It's also unwise to repeat a routine message funeral after funeral. Each funeral is different, and each one demands a personal touch.

In your devotional reading of the Bible, you will come upon texts that will shout at you, "Preach me!" Add these to your notebook or sermon file. (As mentioned earlier, Andrew W. Blackwood called this the "sermonic seed-plot.") In time, as you meditate and serve, the Spirit will mature the text into a message. Pastors who are walking with God will always have that "word in season" from the Spirit (Isa. 50:4). As you grow in your own spiritual life, you will stop using some messages and prepare many new ones. Some texts will be especially meaningful to you, and you will use them more often.

This may sound morbid, but if you have elderly people in your church, or members who are hospitalized or have terminal illnesses, ask God to give you the message their loved ones will need, and be prepared before the person dies. There is no need to be in a panic if the person has been lingering for weeks. We would not tell our people that we have funeral messages prepared for them, but we would pray and plan in advance. This especially holds true for the pillars in the church and the faithful officers. Newspaper offices have their prepared obituaries for great people; pastors can have sermon ideas maturing for their people.

AM I EXPECTED TO ATTEND THE FUNERALS OF RELATIVES OF OUR CHURCH MEMBERS, PEOPLE WHO THEMSELVES WEREN'T A PART OF OUR CHURCH FAMILY?

As their shepherd, you minister primarily (but not exclusively) to those in the church family, and you can do this whether or not you conduct their loved one's service. We've found it helpful to make a ministry visit in the home and then to stop briefly during the visitation time, if there is one. Most of your people wouldn't expect you to attend the funeral, but they might appreciate a visit sometime during the week after the funeral. If one of your members in the family asks to see you, there may be some problem that needs solving, so be available. As we mentioned before, grief has a way of opening up old wounds, creating guilt, and setting the stage for conflict. If the matter is serious and spreads, you and the officiating pastor may want to get together privately for prayer and consultation.

We suggest you have a "bereavement" column in the worship folder or church paper that mentions the families in the church that have experienced the loss of loved ones.

What about "memorial services" and cremation?

More and more families seem to be asking for private burial of their loved one, followed by a public memorial service. The burial is what says "it is finished—this is closure" and it's a very difficult time. But once the committal is over, it's easier for the family and friends to participate in a memorial service that honors the deceased and glorifies the Lord. You don't have to worry about the clock and you won't keep the cemetery staff waiting.

However, don't allow the memorial service to get out of hand, because then it will do more harm than good. The family should plan the service just as they would plan a traditional funeral. The difference is that the memorial service allows more people to speak, it is more flexible and perhaps the atmosphere is more relaxed. The danger is that some garrulous relatives and friends may take over and use up too much time. If you as pastor must follow a long line of such talkative people, your text may have to be John 10:8—"All who ... came before me were thieves and robbers ..."

As for cremation, it's becoming more acceptable among believers, especially in areas where burial space is limited. People used to opt for cremation because the costs were lower than those of traditional burial, but that's changing and the expenses involved in cremation have increased. Many sincere believers associate cremation with pagan practices and feel that cremation isn't a good Christian witness. Cremation accomplishes in a few hours what nature does in sixty or seventy years, and we have bodies embalmed mainly for the purpose of public viewing, not to preserve them indefinitely. Bodies eventually turn to dust.

We believe in the resurrection of the dead, but resurrection is not reconstruction. If a body is cremated and the ashes are scattered, or even kept in an urn in a columbarium, this will make no difference when Jesus returns. We will receive new bodies; there will be continuity but not identity, just like the flower that comes from the planted seed (John 12:23; 1 Cor. 15:35–58). Since salvation involves the whole person—spirit, soul, and body (1 Thess. 5:23)—we show respect to the body both in life and in death. However, we must take care lest a funeral be so "body centered" that we forget the message of life in Christ Jesus.

NOTES

_____
_____
_____
_____
_____
_____
_____

REFLECTIONS

_____
_____
_____
_____
_____
_____
_____

ACTION POINTS

_____
_____
_____
_____
_____
_____
_____

Chapter TWELVE

Fellow Laborers

*What's my relationship to former pastors
of the church, especially my
immediate predecessor?*

Stories about former pastors are often like stories about mothers-in-law: they are only stories. Make up your mind that you will not become envious of any other servant of God and that you will never consider a former pastor a threat to your ministry. It sometimes takes much grace to achieve this, but it is essential if you want to succeed.

To begin with, keep in mind that there is no competition in the Lord's work: we are all laborers together with God. No two pastors have the same gifts, achieve the same goals, or minister in the same ways, but God can still use both of them. One plows, another sows, another waters, another harvests, but it is God that gives the increase (1 Cor. 3:3–9). So your first step toward getting along with your predecessor is to develop a clear understanding of the meaning of the ministry. He has his gifts and (we trust) has used them to make a contribution to the church. You have your gifts and will use them to continue to build the church. The next pastor will come and make his unique contribution.

Always say something good about your predecessors. When members praise them, encourage their praise. Even if your predecessors were failures in some areas (and aren't we all?), find something good to say about them. Do this sincerely and not as a gimmick to make friends and influence people. If you are praying for your immediate predecessor, as you ought to be, you will have no problems.

When you hear criticism, try to cover it with love and kindness. The member who criticizes a former pastor will likely criticize you when you leave, or perhaps before you leave. Let it be known that you will not tolerate unjust criticism. After awhile, it will probably stop.

Make friends with your predecessor if at all possible. If he is a man of God, he will not invade your field, visit your people, and deliberately cause trouble. But you can't help but expect him to want to see people if he visits the area, especially if they love one another. Professional ethics would demand that he contact you first, but not all pastors know about ethics. Each pastor will have two or three families in the church with whom he was especially friendly; no good can come from trying to break up these friendships. Trust your predecessor not to cause problems. He should be wise enough not to visit the field too soon after you arrive, unless invited by the church. If he suggests visiting too soon, don't hesitate to tell him you would rather he wait. Openness and love usually prevail among people who walk with God.

The former pastor can be of help to you but don't run to him with all your problems. Some of these problems he may have helped to cause. Furthermore, you don't want to start your ministry adopting his prejudices and viewpoints. Getting a rundown on all the members of the church could be the worst thing to happen to a new pastor. If this pastoral gossip starts, lovingly suggest that it not continue. This doesn't mean he cannot warn you about serious troublemakers (2 Tim. 4:14–15), but it does mean that he should refrain from sharing his likes and dislikes and expecting you to imitate him.

What about the older pastor who retires and stays on the field? This is a special situation that requires an extra measure of grace. If your predecessor's ministry was long and fruitful, and the people loved him, be very thankful and share this love. Minister to your predecessor in love and he will be a help to you. Also, your love for him will help to win the love of the church family. The instant any jealousy or friction appears, take it to the Lord and settle it. Otherwise your whole ministry will be poisoned, and this can lead to disaster. If the people prefer a former pastor to conduct weddings and funerals, be patient. Suggest that you open the service, or share some other way, but be willing for him to serve. In due time you will win the love and respect of your people.

When the right opportunity comes along, invite your predecessor to come back to preach. But keep in mind that not everyone will agree with this idea, because leaders have enemies as well as friends. Make it a happy occasion of homecoming and you will reap benefits in the years to come.

What do we do when the former pastor left under a dark cloud, perhaps even open sin? Quietly investigate the situation and come to your own conclusion. You have every right to talk to your predecessor and get his point of view. If there was a serious breach of morals, then you must be cautious in your friendship lest you open up old church wounds. You can certainly be a friend and Christian brother, but this doesn't mean you will necessarily invite your predecessor back to preach or encourage the people to reopen the case. No doubt the former minister will be happy if you let the dust lie.

Someday, *you* will be the former pastor, so be careful how you act today. It may not be easy, particularly if your successor seems to be tearing down what you worked so hard to build up, but leave it with God and don't meddle. Especially, don't write letters and don't believe all the gossip. Pray for the church and your successor and plow your own field.

TO WHAT EXTENT SHOULD I FELLOWSHIP WITH OTHER PASTORS IN MY AREA, ESPECIALLY THOSE WHO DON'T SEEM FAITHFUL TO THE WORD OF GOD?

The word fellowship means "to have in common" and you certainly have little in common with a preacher who isn't converted or who doesn't accept the Bible as God's Word. However, this doesn't mean you should treat him like an enemy. It's possible to be friendly with him and even to help him better understand the Word, but you don't want to compromise your testimony in any way. Kindness is always in order, even when you disagree.

If you limit your friendship and fellowship only to the group to which you belong, you may die of loneliness and rob yourself of enrichment. If a pastor is born again and seeks to serve Christ, regardless of what his denominational ties may be, you can fellowship with him. In fact, he may need you as much as you need him. The test of fellowship is Jesus Christ, his person, and work (1 John 4:1–6), not our own interpretations of God's truth. Just about every major denomination today has its evangelicals and its liberals, and we are better off judging (in the best sense) ministers by what they are rather than judging on the basis of what they belong to.

Before we conclude that our own group is the only one that is pure, let's remember that there was a Judas among the Twelve, and even Peter didn't know Judas was of the Devil (John 6:66–71). Before we reject those who don't belong to our special group, let's read Christ's admonition in Mark 9:38–41. We may think that our local church is the only true church in town, but in Revelation 2 and 3, Jesus called groups "churches" that had serious flaws and weaknesses.

It's been our experience that we need the fellowship of other pastors. The pastorate is a difficult work, and God's servants can help to hold up one another's arms as we fight the battle together. We recognize the fact that there is a difference between acquaintanceship, friendship, and fellowship, and that having a cup of coffee with a pastor friend is not quite the same as asking him to preach in your pulpit. You'll find ministers in your area who may not agree with you on every detail of theology but whose fellowship will enrich your life and ministry. Get to know them; pray for them; pray with them. Major on the important facets of the faith, not the minor things. Learn to listen and you will learn from them.

Even where churches may not be able to cooperate with each other in ministry, pastors can still be friends. The unsaved people in our communities enjoy nothing better than beholding wars among pastors and churches. Some pastors thrive on such activities and even build their crowds by attacking other people publicly. We should certainly defend the faith, but let's make doctrines, not people, the focus of attention. And, pastors have a way of moving on; so be patient with your problem neighbor.

WHAT ARE THE GUIDELINES FOR BUILDING AND WORKING WITH A CHURCH STAFF?

As a church grows, the pastor needs more help. It's estimated that the average pastor can do his best with about two hundred people, and after that, he needs help if he wants to avoid a breakdown. Usually the first staff member to be added is a full-time secretary, then an assistant pastor. Ask God to give you a secretary from your church family if possible. If one isn't available, perhaps a sister church in the area has a dedicated member who can serve.

Don't add too many staff members at one time; it takes time for the church family to assimilate new leaders. A staff-run church can turn into a staff-ruined church if the officers and members are left out. You don't want the church to get the idea that the congregation pays the staff and the staff does all the work. The purpose of a pastoral staff is the equipping of the people to do the work of ministry (Eph. 4:7–16).

As you add staff members, be sure to spell out precisely in writing the responsibilities of the ministry, the financial package, to whom the worker is accountable, and the various benefits involved. Be sure to be businesslike in these early steps of expansion, because they will set the pattern for staff additions in the future. Also, keep in mind that a church *calls* staff people; it doesn't *hire* them—unless you want hirelings! They accept a ministry, not a job.

The three basic factors in leadership are responsibility, accountability, and privilege. Every staff member must be accountable to somebody else, usually the senior pastor or a church personnel committee. The more supervision staff members require, the less valuable they are; so call people who can be trusted. If you don't balance responsibility with privilege, you may break your staff people; so don't micromanage the work. Too much privilege means no work is being done; too much responsibility means the worker is getting frustrated. There must be balance.

You should spend time personally with staff members and give them opportunity to share their problems and plans. Don't permit the church's ministry to become problem-centered; it must be purpose-centered. Problems are only opportunities for you to see God at work, and the staff ought to have solutions to suggest. It is good for staff members to give regular reports of their ministry. This helps to keep the staff up-to-date on each other's activities.

As you add staff members, or replace them, beware of simply "assigning jobs." Job descriptions are helpful, but they aren't the last word in administration. In the ministry, we match spiritual gifts and natural abilities to opportunities and needs. For example, each youth pastor will have a different approach in working with young people; one will use sports, another music, and so on. To expect new workers to do exactly the same thing their predecessors did is to embalm the program. You can never duplicate workers, but you can discover gifts and give opportunity for their use. The pastor's task is to create the kind of challenge and atmosphere that will make it easy and exciting for the staff to discover, develop, and use their gifts.

One of the hardest things a pastor must do is deal with a staff member who isn't doing the job. We would like to postpone such a meeting, but we dare not, for the person's sake and for the church's sake. "Wounds from a friend can be trusted" (Prov. 27:6). You must pastor your staff as well as the members of the church. If you have a set schedule for meeting with the staff members individually, you can bring the matter up. If not, you must ask to meet at an opportune time. It will be painful at first, but God will go to work and you two can face the problem and start to find a solution. Never permit your close personal relationship with a staff member to blind you to his or her personal deficiencies.

A pastor with a growing staff carries many burdens that the pastor working alone doesn't encounter. It takes time to work with a staff, and time is a precious commodity in the ministry. Ideally, the time you invest with your staff enables all of you to get more work done. If this isn't the case, something is wrong. A worker's value is indicated by the amount of supervision he or she requires. If you must do all the thinking for your staff members, they are of little value to you.

Many pastors find it helpful to meet with their staff first thing Monday morning. The previous Lord's Day is fresh in their minds and they can share what they have learned about the flock. Go over the week's schedule and make sure there are no conflicts. Update the lists of the names of the sick, the shut-ins, and those in the hospital, and assign calls. An hour or so spent with your staff at the beginning of the week will save you hours of extra work later in the week. It goes without saying that you and your staff will pray together, not only at the weekly staff meeting but frequently during the week as you work together.

Have definite regulations for the staff: lunch hours, coffee breaks, expense accounts, and so on. All of these items should be approved by the necessary official boards of the church. In other words, manage the staff and the office just the way it would be run if it were a business office and not a church office. "But everything should be done in a fitting and orderly way" (1 Cor. 14:40). We must remind our staff members that they're working for the Lord, and that the Lord expects them to be as faithful in the use of their time as if they worked for General Motors or IBM. Set a definite time for all of you to be in the office in the morning. You must set the example and get there earlier. We owe it to the Lord and to our people (whose sacrificial gifts support us) to be faithful and to work hard.

Some senior pastors get upset because they think they work harder than their staff members. Ideally, a staff member exists so that the pastor can get more done, but this may not always be true. Just about the time you need your assistant, he's not there. (Of course, the opposite would be worse—a staff member who works harder than the pastor!) Don't be critical; you don't always know the effective ways your staff members are ministering. If you feel you can't trust them, then you owe them a frank admission of your concern. But don't expect young, beginning assistants to have the same sense of urgency and concern that you have. Occasionally, there are exceptions, but for the most part, our assistants will never discover the full scope of the work until they get churches of their own. If we've built into them the basics of the ministry, they will make it.

One final word: there is a difference between delegating responsibility and passing the buck. Staff members resent it when a pastor shoves onto them the disagreeable tasks he doesn't want to do. Let's be fair with them and treat them as ministers and not "gofers." When we delegate responsibility, we are giving fellow workers a chance to develop their gifts. We keep in touch; we encourage; we provide the backstop when there are problems. Passing the buck means getting something out of our way and forgetting about it.

Chapter THIRTEEN

Dealing with Problem People

How do we deal with "odd" people who gravitate to churches and waste our time with their problems? How can we help them?

Someone has said, "Where the light shines the brightest, the bugs come flying in." A strong Bible ministry and a happy crowd will often attract strange people, especially in a city church. Here are a few practical suggestions.

In almost every church, there are people with problems, people who manufacture problems, and problem people who seem to thrive on their problems. Be kind and loving but honest and firm. Treat these people as Jesus would, and speak the truth in love. Let them know you welcome them in the name of Jesus, but that you can't devote your whole attention to them. Ask them to pray for you, and greet them when you see them. See in them their good qualities and not necessarily their bad ones. Remember what our Lord said about "the least of these brothers of mine" (Matt. 25:40. See also v. 45).

Often these people will descend on you after a service when you want to talk to other visitors or to people who were touched by the Word. Here is where godly church members can perform a great ministry. Have two or three of your good men and women standing near you, and let them rescue you when the conversation gets too long.

They can say, "Pastor, we hate to interrupt you, but there's a woman here who has a spiritual problem. Perhaps we could chat with Mr. Jones while you speak to her." This can be done graciously without embarrassing anyone.

These people often have real needs and sometimes serious emotional problems, so seek to minister to their needs but never permit them to monopolize your time. They may not know how to spell codependence but they can practice it! Don't attempt to be an amateur psychiatrist. Introduce them to strong Christians in the church who know how to help such people. You never can tell what your ministry of kindness will mean to them in their lonely hours.

Sometimes people will approach you after a service, asking you to endorse a book or product, or to explain some long difficult passage in the Bible. Suggest that they phone you during the week, or make a definite appointment right then and there. Explain that the church doesn't endorse products and that the official board handles such matters. But keep in mind that these seemingly out-of-place requests may cover a deeper need. The person may want to approach you but doesn't quite know how. Some of your greatest opportunities for ministry may be found in situations that seem awkward to you. No doubt when Jesus was on earth, he was approached by all kinds of problem people, and we have every reason to believe that he received them kindly and sought to meet their needs. We should do likewise.

There are people whose only mark of identity is that they live with the same perpetual problem, but if you helped them solve that problem, they'd lose their identity. They probably don't want the problem solved. These people need professional help, but most of them would deny it and refuse to see a counselor.

MOST CHURCHES SEEM TO HAVE AT LEAST ONE RESIDENT CRITIC OR "BOSS." WHAT'S THE STRATEGY IN HANDLING THEM?

If the church is growing, these problem people may soon be lost in the crowd. They're "big frogs" as long as the puddle is small and shallow. Deepen the waters and they may drown. All of which means: without being unkind, don't focus your attention on the problem people. Focus it on the dedicated people and the leaders who want to build the church. If when you stand up to preach you see only the critics and the would-be "church boss," your ministry is in danger of becoming sour and defensive. Feed the people. As the body grows, it will better be able to fight off the germs.

When the situation calls for it, face critics lovingly and honestly. Don't wait for a crisis. Ask God to give you wisdom, and you will know just when to deal with the issue privately. Each church needs a leader, and if that leader is somebody other than the chosen pastor, then they don't need the pastor. Make up your mind that with God's help you will lead the flock.

Most critics and church dictators cannot face facts honestly in Christian love, so your openness will disarm them. Christ's instructions in Matthew 18:15–20 must be kept in mind. We would hope that these situations wouldn't develop into matters for discipline, but be prepared just the same.

Often church critics have been wounded and their inflated egos won't permit the wound to heal. Perhaps a former pastor hurt them, and now they're protecting themselves from further hurt by criticizing the new pastor. Sometimes it doesn't hurt pastors to have critics in the field. It helps to keep them alert and encourages them to do a better job. If everyone speaks well of us, we may backslide and become self-sufficient and proud, and that way lies failure.

The "church boss" is as old as the church itself. John wrote about Diotrephes, "who loves to be first" (3 John 9). Some church bosses are bossed at home or on the job, and they use the church as a means of building their own ego. These people have personality problems as well as spiritual problems, and you must handle them carefully. Perhaps God will use your preaching to help them recover. Above all else, pray for them. Usually the good people of the church are glad to have a pastor who will handle the boss in a sane, biblical manner. It may take months, or even years, before the boss will challenge your leadership;

but if you have been ministering in the Spirit, you will be able to operate from a position of strength and authority. Be firm, be loving, and don't be afraid. Better to face the battle and win than to keep avoiding it and develop ulcers.

Handle these matters the way you plan to handle all such matters, and the message will get around.

WHAT DO WE DO ABOUT ANONYMOUS LETTERS AND PHONE CALLS?

Ignore them.

Always look at the signature on a letter first. If there is none, hand the letter to your secretary or to a trusted associate to read. If there is anything in the letter you should know, they can tell you. If you read every anonymous letter that comes, you'll get agitated and angry, and Satan will use this to hurt your ministry. People who can help you in your work won't hide behind anonymity. People who love you and trust you will talk to you personally, even if they disagree with you. If a letter's not worth signing, it's not worth reading.

Phone calls are a bit more difficult. If you have a secretary, he or she can screen them by saying, "May I ask who is calling?" If the person refuses to tell, your secretary can inform you, and you can take the call or refuse it as you feel led. The great problem is this: needy people will often phone a pastor for help, but they want to remain anonymous. This is especially true in metropolitan areas. If you take the call, ask "What can I do to help you?" and seek to determine whether the caller is a crank, a critic, or a needy case. If the caller is either of the first two, simply say, 'Well, I'm afraid I can't help you, but let me pray for you," and as soon as you finish the prayer, hang up. If the person is really in need, stay on the line and try to help. Seek to establish confidence so you can suggest a personal conference. More than one desperate person has been saved from suicide by a pastor who took time to listen, love, and pray.

If you have no secretary, you must do your own screening. Experience helps here; so does firmness. Don't get agitated, don't argue and don't carry on long meaningless conversations. Above all else, don't carry the conversation around with you and get so uptight nobody can live with you. That is exactly what Satan wants. Commit the conversation to the Lord and go back to your work.

WHAT SHOULD I DO WHEN PEOPLE LEAVE THE CHURCH IN A HUFF BECAUSE THEY'RE ANGRY AT SOMEONE OR SOMETHING? SHOULD WE TRY TO WIN THEM BACK OR JUST BE THANKFUL THAT THEY'RE GONE?

Nobody should be forced to stay in a church or be bribed to come back. Matthew 18:15–17 certainly applies here. If something that you said or did caused people to leave, go to them privately to try to straighten it out. If they refuse, take two or three spiritual saints with you for another visit. If the offended person still refuses to talk it over, take it to the church and let the whole body settle it.

Church members who leave in a huff are usually saying, like little children in a baseball game, "If I can't run things my way, I'll take my bat and ball and go home!" They really believe that their absence is going to wreck the church, and they probably hope that it will. No doubt they've done the same thing in three or four other churches in town. We call them "the nomads"—they get mad, say no, and off they go! It's unfortunate that we have such carnal Christians in our churches, but we do, and we must face them honestly but lovingly.

Don't encourage such people to come back. Don't bargain with them or make concessions. If you do, they'll do the same thing the next time something bothers them. Very likely the spiritual people in the church will stand with you in the matter because they're weary of seeing their church run and ruined by immature members. (Of course, where there are relatives, the attitude may be different.) If you are new in the church, your spiritual men can give you the background of the problem.

Always be kind to these people; otherwise you will give them ammunition for their crusade. If you should see them, greet them, but don't give the impression that you're anxious to win them back. Pray for them. Don't talk about them except in official board meetings; otherwise the church gossips will add fuel to the fire. You may live to see the day when God will really deal with them and bring them to a place of spiritual usefulness.

Some churches have an escape clause in their constitution that helps to take care of situations like this. It says: "After becoming a member of this church, if we find something that we disagree with in either the doctrine or practice of the church, we promise to ask to have our names removed from the roll." This permits disgruntled people to remove themselves, and also saves you the problems of further investigation and possible discipline. This clause is not a substitute for church discipline; rather, it is an attempt to obey Romans 12:18: "If it is possible, as far as it depends on you, live at peace with everyone." By the way, their request for removing their names from the church roll must be in writing.

Church discipline is a subject that's more avoided than applied, yet it needs to be applied if the church is to glorify God. We'll discuss it in chapter 15.

How do we break up church cliques?

We want our church members to know, love, and enjoy each other, so be sure it is really a clique and not simply a group of good friends who love each other and enjoy doing things together. Only when a group of members isolates itself from the rest of the church and seeks to become a power bloc do you have a clique.

Cliques are formed in several ways. Sometimes there is a strong member who naturally attracts people and influences them. Or, there may be a problem in the church that needs solving, and people start to take sides. Some of these problems have long histories and deep roots and the cliques have been there a long time.

If you feel you have a clique in your church, immerse yourself in Paul's letter to the Philippians. Some were for him, some were against him, and some wouldn't commit themselves. Note how the apostle loved them all ("all of you" is a key phrase in the letter) and tried to get them all to love Christ and one another. Jesus himself set the example of humility and patience that we must imitate. Unless the issue involves a serious matter of church policy or doctrine, don't preach about it from the safety of the pulpit. Be a peacemaker, pray for them all, love them all, and watch for opportunities to pull down walls and start building bridges. Always find something good to say about all who are involved. Keep the bigger issues before the people: winning the lost, sending out missionaries, building the church for which Jesus died. Let the Spirit of God show them their own pettiness, selfishness, and lack of vision.

It sometimes takes a crisis to melt people's hearts, and sometimes it's the pastor who must suffer. No matter: our Savior suffered for us, and we're privileged to share in the fellowship of his sufferings. Wait, watch, pray, love people, and preach the Word positively. God will work and you will have the joy of seeing progress. Perhaps the whole problem may not be solved during your ministry, but you will have helped the next pastor solve it.

Some churches, unfortunately, have built-in divisions that no pastor has been able to remove. We know of one church where an entire Sunday school class refused to accept the new pastor, and went right on functioning by itself, totally apart from the rest of the church. The wise pastor learns to smile at such attitudes, love all the people, and seek to be a blessing to them all. You can't force people to like you, and they can't force you to hate them. You can pray for them and ask God to make them what they ought to be. Don't allow the smallness of the few to rob you of the love of the many. Just as the human body sometimes has to function in spite of a weakness or an injury, so the spiritual body must function even though it suffers from broken bones. (By the way, the word "restore" in Galatians 6:1 means "to set a broken bone.") If you have to live with such a division, accept it and do the best you can. God knows, God cares, and God will work it out in his time.

ONE OF OUR MEMBERS HAS SOME PECULIAR VIEWS ABOUT SCRIPTURE, AND HE TRIES TO CONVERT NEW MEMBERS TO HIS VIEWS. WHAT SHOULD I DO?

After you have formed a good relationship, go to the member personally and lovingly and discuss these views. If they are definitely unscriptural, then try to instruct in the truth (2 Tim. 2:23–26). The problem may be ignorance, so be patient. If the member is definitely holding to unscriptural teachings and refuses to repent, you will have to take whatever official action is necessary (Rom. 16:17–20). Sometimes people like this have read a few books and their knowledge has inflated their ego instead of melting their heart (1 Cor. 8:1).

The word *heretic* (Titus 3:10 KJV) carries with it the meaning of "one who makes a choice." That is, there are people in the church who want others to make a choice for them or against them, as if their views are the only views. Heretics divide the church and Titus 3:9–11 tells us what to do with these people. They should be warned twice and the third time should be officially dismissed from the church and not received back.

For some reason, just about every church has people who "dig deep into the Word" and come up with unusual interpretations. If these views are insignificant, ignore them. This may be their only way to get attention. Instead of using their time to win the lost or edify the saints, like the cultists, these people only try to win converts to their cause. Most of the time these members are harmless and the church smiles at them and ignores them. However, they may become real problems and must be dealt with. Let them know you love them but disagree with them and can't permit them to infect the church. Talk to them in private and patiently try to reason with them. If they won't listen, then you have no alternative but to protect the church by disciplining them.

Chapter FOURTEEN

Membership

How does a church maintain an honest membership roll? To say we have three hundred (or three thousand) members when we can't locate half of them is, to me, deceitful. We don't want a lot of inactive members, but at the same time, we don't want to anger a lot of people who consider themselves members.

One way to maintain clean membership lists is simply to put into your constitution: "Every six months, the pastor and deacons (elders) shall examine the church roll. Members who have not attended for six months shall automatically be put on an inactive roll. If they return and begin to attend faithfully, they shall then be put back on the active roll." This requirement for active membership should be explained to all present members and to new members when they join, and their acceptance of membership is proof that they agree with it. Nobody should join the church with his eyes closed.

The church entrusts to the pastor and deacons (elders) this privilege of reviewing the church roll. A group of faithful people will know better who has been attending church than would a lone officer. The pastor doesn't have to read the names publicly and embarrass everybody. It also means that delinquent members are not put out of the church but simply put into a different category. If they go to another church and ask for a letter of transfer, the letter states: "On July 5, 1992, by order of the deacons, Mr. John Jones was placed on the inactive roll." Again, we must emphasize that this policy should be explained to all new members.

How do you notify members of their change in status? Actually, the pastor and deacons (and Sunday school teachers) ought to be tracking down inactive members all year long. A personal visit is in order if you know where the member lives. (Sometimes, inactive members move away and leave no forwarding address. In this case, do the best you can to find them and direct them to a good church.) Remind them of everyone's need for spiritual nourishment and fellowship and that in a few weeks they could lose their full membership. Be patient, be kind, be prayerful, and don't be in such a hurry that you see only a list of names and not individuals who need Christ's love.

It's usually unwise to send these members letters of warning. A letter can be a cold, impersonal thing, and if it's received at a time when the member is upset, it can do damage. Furthermore, a member out of fellowship with the Lord can carry the letter all over town, show it to people and hurt the reputation of the church. These absentee members deserve a visit, and that should not be the last visit. Keep in touch with them because you never can tell what God may do.

All of this demands personal concern and attention on the part of pastor and leaders, but it's worth it. We are members of the body of Christ, and as such, we must minister to each other. The church that cares for individuals is the church that grows.

It may take a few years for you to get such an arrangement in your church program, so be patient. When your members realize that such a policy doesn't slam the door on members, nor does it embarrass people, they will readily accept it. Church membership should be a valuable, meaningful thing, and this is one way to accomplish that.

The big problem comes, of course, when the church is voting on an important matter and one group rounds up all the inactive members to help support their cause. Do the best you can to maintain an honest church membership roll, but don't expect this to solve every problem.

How does a pastor go about building church loyalty? So many parachurch organizations are asking for the time, money, and energy of my good members that I hardly know how to compete.

Feed your sheep and love them. God will give you spiritual ties that will be stronger than the ties another organization can manufacture. Don't criticize other groups; God is using many of them in wonderful ways. In fact, if all our churches were busy doing what God wants done, many of these groups would never have been organized.

The biggest mistake many pastors make is failing to involve their people meaningfully in the local church. Mature Christians with talents and spiritual gifts want to go to work. If the local church does not use them, some other group will. The growing edge of your local church is with the new converts, so put them to work. Of course, new believers are not ready yet to teach a class or serve as deacons, but they can go visiting and start sharing their faith. They can work in the church and use their abilities for the Lord. In most cases, the new Christian is bubbling over with energy, and that energy must be directed into challenging ministries.

Some church members prefer to work in parachurch organizations for reasons that we consider less than Christian. There is more prestige, for one thing. In the local church, we try not to put people on pedestals. Furthermore, there is usually more freedom and less discipline in outside organizations. Whiz kids who get frustrated by church policies and procedures sometimes escape to outside organizations where they can do what they please and be praised for it. You can be thankful if they are not a part of your official family.

On the other hand, many fine, loyal church members feel it is God's will for them to serve in other organizations. These people will be loyal to you and to the church, but they may not always be present at meetings. Their ministry will take them elsewhere. Fine! Perhaps they are doing more good sharing Christ in another church than sitting listening to you. Don't be upset; show an interest in their ministry, pray for them, and be thankful they are busy for the Lord.

Get to know the leaders of these parachurch organizations. Some of them might be a blessing to you. Don't be afraid to disagree with them, but disagree in the right spirit.

In your ministry, emphasize to your people the importance of the local church. (It is interesting that some parachurch organizations that often criticize the church go to the church for their support.) Organizations come and go, rise and fall, but the local church goes on. Its work might not be as exciting as that of some other group, but it may be more lasting. As your own ministry of the Word blesses the people, they will come because they are being fed. Keep the church program moving; plan ahead; keep them involved. Let them know often that you love and appreciate them. In time, their hearts will be knit together and they will love their church and support it.

HOW MUCH TIME SHOULD I SPEND WITH MEMBERS WHO DON'T SUPPORT THE CHURCH OR MY MINISTRY? SHOULDN'T I SPEND MORE TIME WITH THE FAITHFUL MEMBERS?

Ephesians 4:7–16 teaches that the pastor's task is to equip the saints to do the work of the ministry, but you can't equip people who are outside the influence of your ministry. We must always emphasize winning the lost and equipping the saints, because this is what builds the church. But this doesn't mean that we ignore the fringe members or the people we think are only spectators.

Get to know them, visit them on occasion, and pray for them faithfully. As Paul reminds us (1 Cor. 12:14–26), the person we think is useless to the church may be indispensable to the work. One day God may give you a real opportunity to challenge that person, and you'll be glad you kept the door open; or, you may be called to conduct their funeral, and you'll be glad you kept in contact.

We can't prove this statistically, but it seems that there are three groups in every church. The top 10 or 15 percent will be spiritual if there's no pastor—these are the pillars of the church. The bottom 10 percent wouldn't serve God if the apostle Paul were their pastor. The middle 75 percent will go one way or the other. Now, if you invest quality time with the top 10 or 15 percent, they can reach down and pull up the 75 percent. (This is Ephesians 4 in practice.) And as the 75 percent start to move, they will touch some in that lower 10 percent. In other words, it may be that some of your members can do a better job encouraging the fringe members than the pastor can. Let them accept the challenge.

Please don't spend all your time trying to rescue the few, and don't permit them to rob you of precious time that belongs to the faithful. The healthy sheep reproduce after their kind, so keep them healthy.

AT WHAT AGE SHOULD CHILDREN BE PERMITTED TO JOIN THE CHURCH?

In churches of the Reformed tradition, children become communicant members at baptism and then are received into full membership at confirmation. The procedure varies from group to group and even from church to church. We will discuss the problem as it relates to the churches that receive their members on profession of faith. Of course, any prospective member ought to be able to give a personal testimony of his faith in Christ, regardless of what the membership procedure may be.

The issue is not so much age as maturity, and "child differeth from child in maturity." Just as children are not all the same size at the same age, so they don't all have the same spiritual perception at the same age. To receive a child who is too young to know what membership is about is to rob that child of a richer spiritual experience at a later time. Anyone who has worked with teenagers knows the recurring problem: "I was supposed to have been saved when I was six, but now I'm not so sure."

Too often, Christian parents push their youngsters into decisions and in later years the children rebel. Every pastor has heard the plea of the doting mother: "Oh, please take Junior in! You should hear him pray at the table! We just know God is going to make a missionary out of him!" In later years, Junior too often becomes a mission field instead of a missionary.

Our counsel is to take each individual applicant separately and be sure there's solid evidence of spiritual life and growth. Obviously, a child's expression of faith is not going to be as mature as that of an adult. If it is, beware of deliberate imitation. If the child is truly born again, to postpone baptism and church membership a few years will not destroy his or her soul. Following the biblical pattern of the Jews, many churches set twelve as the minimum age for membership, and this seems a good idea. Children who grow up in Christian homes often show signs of spiritual life earlier. But again, we want to warn against imitation or decisions made simply to please the parents. It is wise to have sixteen as the age for full voting privileges in the church. It is doubtful whether most twelve-year-old members could vote with much intelligence or spiritual discernment.

HOW CAN WE BEST ASSIMILATE NEW MEMBERS INTO THE CHURCH FAMILY?

Present them to the church publicly so that everybody has the opportunity to meet them. Some churches use a new members' reception to do this. Encourage officers to invite the new members into their homes. You and your staff should set the example here.

Use the buddy system (or the Timothy system) and relate the new member to another member of the church (2 Tim. 2:2). They can go calling together, for one thing. Enthusiastic new converts can be the cutting edge of the church, so let them share their faith!

It's unwise to thrust new people suddenly into places of responsibility, because they usually need time to assimilate the church culture. Take the time to discover their gifts and talents, prove them in smaller places, and then match them to a ministry when they're ready. Going to work for the Lord is the best way to feel at home in a church. Alas, some eager pastors push their "converts" into places of leadership and take control of their thinking and serving. This pushes out the older and more experienced people, and before long amateurs *are* the church. See 1 Timothy 3:6 and 5:22.

The ministry of assimilation should not be left to chance. Someone on your staff or among your officers should be appointed to direct this ministry and see to it that no new convert or new member is neglected. A new member with the wrong church friends could become a problem.

We recall a pastor who was emphasizing to his church leaders the importance of evangelism. "We want to see dozens of new converts and new members," he told them. One of the more astute officers replied, "Pastor, that's a noble goal, and we're right with you. But the big question is this: is our church at this time prepared to care for and assimilate that many new babies?" This led to the development of a much-needed assimilation ministry, and God did give them the babies to care for.

NOTES

REFLECTIONS

ACTION POINTS

Chapter FIFTEEN

Church Discipline

*Isn't church discipline legalistic? Aren't
we supposed to practice grace?*

Grace and truth came through Jesus Christ" (John 1:17). Where there is a Christ-honoring, Bible-centered and Spirit-led ministry, there must be truth; for God's Word is truth (John 17:17), Jesus is the truth (John 14:6), and "the Spirit is the truth" (1 John 5:6). Grace doesn't mean we cover up sin or look the other way. Grace means we lovingly deal with sin and apply the cleansing instructions of the Word of God, for grace reigns through righteousness (Rom. 5:21). "Let us do evil that good may result" isn't a Christian approach (Rom. 3:8).

God disciplines his children so that they will become more like Jesus (Heb. 12). However, it's not the discipline of a judge punishing a wicked criminal, but that of a broken-hearted parent helping to mature a beloved child. Yes, church discipline can be practiced in a legalistic, holier-than-thou attitude, but that's not what the Scriptures teach. We are to treat one another the way God treats us, and he's merciful (1 Chron. 21:13) and compassionate (Ps. 103:9–13). If we love the Lord, we will hate what he hates (Ps. 97:10; 139:21–22; Rom. 12:9).

IF CHURCH OFFICERS FALL INTO SERIOUS SIN AND CONFESS IT AND MAKE THINGS RIGHT, SHOULD THEY GIVE UP THEIR OFFICES? IF SO, HOW SOON CAN THEY RETURN TO SERVE?

We know of no place in the New Testament that says believers must be put on probation after making things right with God and their church. Peter confessed his sin and was restored to fellowship and discipleship (John 21:15–19), and he was an apostle!

However, when it comes to spiritual leaders, two factors must be considered: the officer's own spiritual life, and any loss of confidence on the part of others in the church, especially other officers. When we confess our sins, God immediately forgives us, but sometimes there must be a period of "recuperation" before we're ready to serve. Medication that kills the germs doesn't automatically restore the patient's health and strength. To reenter the ministry arena too soon may cause another collapse. If the other officers have doubts, it might be wise to suggest a furlough. This doesn't mean the church rejects the confession; rather, it means the members have too great a love for the offender to let him hurt himself by beginning to carry his spiritual responsibilities too soon.

Try to keep discipline matters from becoming public scandals. The greater the place of responsibility, the greater the damage when the person sins. There will be some cases when the wisest move is for the offender to resign quietly after making things right. If the confession is sincere, the officer will not balk at this suggestion. In situations involving theft, immorality, or defiance of authority, it's best for the offender to resign the office. The pastor will want to assist the member with regular counsel. Remember Paul's counsel that we love and forgive truly repentant believers, lest they get depressed and become the Devil's targets (2 Cor. 2:1–11).

HOW CAN WE BEGIN TO PRACTICE DISCIPLINE IN CHURCHES THAT HAVE IGNORED IT FOR YEARS?

Discipline is an important part of the Christian life, for God disciplines his children (Heb. 12) and we must discipline ourselves

(1 Cor. 9:24–27). God expects the pastor to discipline his own children (1 Tim. 3:4–5), and also to discipline God's children when they need it. Church discipline is actually God's exercising spiritual authority through a local church for the purposes of reclaiming an erring believer and maintaining the purity of the local church.

Begin by talking the matter over with the church leaders before informing the church. In as loving a manner as possible, let the church know that you want to obey the Word. Explain that discipline is an evidence of love. If you love your members, you will want to rescue them from sin. First Corinthians 5 indicates that discipline is exercised for the sake of the offender (1–5), the church (6–8), and the unsaved society that needs the witness of a godly church (9–13). Church discipline isn't a pastor throwing his weight around, or a church board acting like a police court. Church discipline must be God at work in the life of the church, or it will not succeed.

Matthew 18 describes the necessary ingredients for successful discipline: humility (1–6), honesty (15–17), obedience to the Word (18–19), prayer (20), and a forgiving spirit (21–35). Unless a church has the right spiritual atmosphere, attempts at discipline will do more harm than good. Before you can even begin to start practicing it, you must get the church into the right spiritual condition, and this takes time, prayer, love, and faithful teaching.

Who should handle discipline? It begins with a concerned pastor (Heb. 13:17; 1 Peter 5:1–4). First Timothy 5 advises that we pastors treat our people like members of the family: the older members as fathers and mothers, the younger as brothers and sisters (vv. 1–2). We advise the pastor to take the first step privately and see the offender. Later, other leaders can be involved. Most churches have procedures laid down either in the denomination's book of discipline or in the constitution; but these principles should not prevent the pastor from privately meeting with suspected offenders and seeking to help them. It has been our experience that offenders are relieved when the pastor, in love, talks to them privately, friend to friend, and seeks to restore them.

Of course, if our private interview does not help, then Galatians

6:1–3 comes into play: take some spiritual leaders from the church and try again. Jesus said the same thing in Matthew 18. If this doesn't work, then the whole church (unfortunately) must be involved (see 1 Cor. 5). When sin is not confessed, it has a way of growing and involving more people. Here are some guidelines:

1. Before you make any serious accusations, be sure you have witnesses (1 Tim. 5:19; 2 Cor. 13:1). You want facts, not rumors.
2. If the case is especially serious or the offender hostile, take witnesses with you when you make that first contact.
3. Try to be impartial (1 Tim. 5:21).
4. Don't jump the gun! Read Proverbs 18:13, 17 and 1 Timothy 5:22. Take time to pray, think, and wait; but don't permit caution to keep you from acting. Don't expect to be aware of everything involved (1 Tim. 5:24–25).

WHAT OFFENSES SHOULD BE CONSIDERED SERIOUS ENOUGH TO REQUIRE DISCIPLINE?

As we see them, these offenses should require church intervention and possible discipline:

1. Personal difference between two or more members (Matt. 18:15–18; Phil. 4:1–3). Don't pry into personal feuds until at least one person involved has tried to obey Christ's instructions.
2. Refusal to earn a living (2 Thess. 3:6–16; 1 Tim. 5:8).
3. Doctrinal error. Begin with patient teaching (2 Tim. 2:23–26); if this fails, use rebuke (Titus 1:10–14; Gal. 2:14). The final step is avoiding the person (Rom. 16:17–18) and rejecting him or her from the fellowship (2 John 9–11). Exercise discernment with people who have doctrinal problems. There's a difference between ignorance of the

Word and promoting false teaching when the person already knows the truth.

4. Repeated troublemaking (Titus 3:10). People who canvass the church membership asking, "Are you on my side or the preacher's side?" should be given two warnings; the third time, they should be dismissed from the fellowship.

5. Open sin (1 Cor. 5; Gal. 6:1–3). The attitude of the church must be that of mourning that such a thing should ever happen. Offenders are given opportunity to repent and make matters right. If they refuse, they must be dismissed. (The Greek word in 1 Cor. 5:2 and 13 means "to expel, to drive out.") This is the official act of the majority of the church (2 Cor. 2:6). Of course, if offenders repent, they can and should be forgiven and received back (2 Cor. 2:6–10).

Some church members think discipline causes trouble, but this is true only if it is carried out in the wrong spirit and without humility and prayer. Loving discipline in a church always unites the family, just as it does in a home. It strengthens the authority of the Word; it honors Christ; it challenges the church to higher levels of spiritual experience. It also strengthens the testimony of the church to outsiders.

Remember the basic principle: private sin, private confession; public sin, public confession. Try not to hang dirty wash out in public. It isn't necessary to explain the sordid details to the whole church, especially with children and teenagers present. If a person comes forward for reinstatement, let the church know that you and the officers have dealt with the matter, and that the person should be forgiven and received. This can be a precious experience of love for both the forgiven offender and the church family.

Like medicine, the best kind of discipline is preventive. When the Word is faithfully preached, the Holy Spirit uses it to convict hearts and exercise discipline. Keep your eyes open for the beginnings of sin, for it's easier to cleanse a wound than to amputate a limb. God gives his shepherds "spiritual radar" that helps them detect when things are starting to go wrong; and at that point, we must act. Pray for God's direction, and at the right time he will give you opportunity to speak to the persons involved. If you handle discipline in the right way, it will make your people love you more, because they know you care too much to permit them to sin. "Wounds from a friend can be trusted, but an enemy multiplies kisses" (Prov. 27:6).

Finally, it's worth noting that you don't use a cannon to kill a flea. Second Thessalonians 3:6–16 suggests degrees of discipline: exhorting (v. 12), holding aloof from offenders (vv. 6, 14), and publicly warning the person (v. 15). Public expulsion is the last resort, and we would trust that offenders would come to their senses before that's necessary. But if discipline is needed, don't be afraid to act. Just be sure your leaders are with you and that you all obey the Word in the spirit of meekness.

What if somebody in the pastor's own family goes wrong and needs discipline?

What our children do after they have matured and left home is not always under our direct control. We believe that if children are raised right, they will be inclined to live right; but more than one Christian worker has had a son or a daughter turn prodigal. And praise God, many of these prodigals eventually find their way back home! Therefore, never give up on anybody. "Love never fails" (1 Cor. 13:8).

One of the requirements for a pastor is that his children be obedient and respectful (1 Tim. 3:4–5), which we assume refers to children who are still at home and under the authority of their parents. We see no reason why a faithful pastor should leave the ministry because an older member of the family has gone wrong. Why have two victims? Do church officers step aside when their children go wrong? Not usually.

We must confess, however, that the ministry can be hurt by the poor testimony of a family member. This may be a burden we will have to live with. If a younger child's behavior really cripples your witness and work, then perhaps you ought to move to a sphere of ministry other than the pastorate. But don't despair. Life isn't over yet and God isn't finished with us.

Often it's not the church members but the fellow pastors who are hardest on the pastor. Let's be loving and forgiving; Matthew 7:1–5 is still in the Bible. Christian love forbids us to record here the names of some great men of God whose children have broken their hearts. For that matter, many a servant of God has seen a new touch of God on his ministry because of the heartache of a family crisis. God is still able to turn "the curse into a blessing" (Neh. 13:2).

NOTES

_____

_____

_____

_____

_____

_____

_____

REFLECTIONS

_____

_____

_____

_____

_____

_____

ACTION POINTS

_____

_____

_____

_____

_____

_____

_____

Chapter SIXTEEN

The Pastor and Home

*To what extent should my spouse
share in my ministry?*

Since in marriage "two become one," your spouse shares in it whether you like it or not. Pastors who can't confide in their spouses and receive help in sharing the load are destined for a lonely and difficult ministry. Our homes often say more to our people than do our sermons. Ministers' homes ought to be quiet benedictions to their neighborhoods and blessings to the churches that they serve.

How much actual ministerial activity your spouse shares in depends on spiritual gifts and special abilities. Some people are quiet and retiring and do their best work behind the scenes, training and encouraging others. Others joyfully accept places of leadership and service in public. Your spouse must be herself/himself and not an imitation of somebody else. If you move to a new ministry, give your spouse time to "settle in" before taking any church responsibilities. Yes, you're a team, but it's not likely both of you will be on the church payroll! Furthermore, your spouse must not become so indispensable to the church that your departure would weaken some ministry or even make it collapse.

The important thing is that both of you fulfill the ministry God has given you, both in the home and in the church. Some members of the church may want to pour you into a mold, but resist it. Your individual ministries will blend and be a blessing when both of you are serving as God has planned. When you find yourself tense and frustrated at home, then both of you must examine your hearts and schedules and see if things are out of balance. As you pray together daily, God will guide you. It is an exciting thing to grow together and serve together in God's work!

This leads to another question: Is it wise for an unmarried person to pastor a church?

Matthew 19:12 indicates that a person's marital status isn't as simple as just going out and finding a mate, and 1 Corinthians 7:7–12 and 32–35 must also be considered. We must all determine God's will for our own life. Better to live in single loneliness than married unhappiness. Or, to put it another way, better to go through life wanting what you don't have than having what you don't want.

But, all things considered, it's wise to seek a mate in the will of God (Gen. 2:18). Many good men have pastored successfully without being married; Phillips Brooks, Clarence F. Macartney, and Robert Murray M'Cheyne come to mind. (Brooks later admitted that his bachelorhood was a big mistake.) But there's something about a vibrant Christian home that enriches character and ministry. The qualifications in 1 Timothy 3 do not demand marriage, but they do assume it.

Many of the problems a pastor must face in the counseling ministry have to do with marriage and the home, so it's good to have firsthand experience of how the Lord helps us in our homes. It's one thing to speak "from authorities" and quite another to speak "with authority," the kind of authority that comes from wholesome personal experience.

Don't make the quest for a mate the central drive of your life. Be the kind of Christian you ought to be and the Lord will do the rest. When the right one comes along, you'll be glad you waited.

You're saying, then, that the minister's home is a vital part of the ministry.

Exactly. The pastor's home is definitely a part of the ministry, but it should not become a part of the church building. The minister's family should have as much privacy as any other member of the church. Should your family have to live next to or very near the church sanctuary, don't allow the members to stop in before church or linger in your home after the service. It may take a few misunderstandings before you get the point across to well-meaning but thoughtless people. No couple can endure being host and hostess seven days a week. Never make plans for the use of your home for a church function without consulting your spouse, unless you want to lose your happy home.

Certainly we ought to use our homes to the glory of God. "Hospitable" is one of the requirements for the ministry (1 Tim. 3:2). Peter gives this same commandment to all church members in 1 Peter 4:8–9, so it must be important.

Whom do we entertain and when? Try to have your officers and their spouses in your home at least once a year. In larger churches where you have many leaders, you may have to schedule several dinners throughout the year. New members appreciate the opportunity of getting to know the pastor better. The youth of the church ought to be included, and remember to invite the college students over when they're home for spring break, holidays, or their summer vacation. Not all of these occasions need to be full-blown dinners. Pizza after church can mean just as much. Try to have the newly engaged couples over as well as the newly married. Give them a living example of a happy Christian home.

Be sure to keep a record of the names of your guests and what was served. Do this not only with your own people but with visiting speakers and missionaries as well. A record saves embarrassment, and it also helps in planning future meals. Knowing what each person likes and dislikes (or is allergic to) will help make you two the ideal host and hostess.

HOW CAN I BE A FAITHFUL MINISTER, SPOUSE, AND PARENT AT THE SAME TIME? HOW DO WE AVOID CONFLICT BETWEEN HOME AND CHURCH?

Conflicts can best be avoided by being one and the same person at all times, your real self and your best self. A happy home and a happy church are made up of the same ingredients: love, discipline, sacrifice, the Word, and prayer. We should be as loving in the church as we are at home, and we should be as disciplined at home as we are at the church. It is when we separate home life from church life that we get into trouble. The pastor must be a person of integrity and not an actor who frequently changes roles. There's no place for pretense in ministry; another word is hypocrisy.

The pastor ministers to the family when ministering to the church and to the church when ministering to the family at home, for a successful Christian home is the greatest strength of the local church. We're always pastors, always spouses, always parents. To say that we're not, or to act as though we're not, is to wear ourselves out changing masks, and one day we'll be discovered.

A pastor must spend time with the family. Family counselors remind us that it is not always the quantity of time but the quality of time that counts. This is probably true, but children can't always tell the difference. You deserve a day off, and you can't spend every evening in a committee meeting. Fortunately, most pastors can arrange their own schedules and prioritize their time. Often it means sacrifice, but life is made up of sacrifices.

If you and your spouse are in accord, the children won't suffer. If one of you is upset because of a demanding schedule, you had both better take time for a personal inventory. If any one of the children begins to show signs of personal problems, reconsider your schedule and perhaps get professional counsel. Each child is different, and some children demand more attention than others. It isn't necessary to sacrifice a child for the success of a church; God can take care of both.

Your personal devotional life and your times of prayer with your spouse are keys to success in this area. The two of you set the atmosphere in the home. Keep alert for signals that tell you it is time for a change in family plans. Nobody enjoys emergencies, but sometimes they're opportunities to examine the dynamics in the family.

HOW CAN YOUNG MALE MINISTERS PROTECT THEMSELVES FROM DESIGNING WOMEN IN A CHURCH?

Two corrections, please: it can happen to women in ministry as well as men, and it can happen to older people as well as younger people. Age has nothing to do with it. More than one mature pastor has fallen in this way, "So, if you think you are standing firm, be careful that you don't fall" (1 Cor. 10:12). If your own marriage is all it ought to be, no person on earth can tempt you. We defeat germs by maintaining good health, and we deal with this particular temptation by maintaining a healthy marriage. If you find yourself thinking sexually about any other person, you had better head for home and start repairing the damage that has already been done there. Your spouse may not always tell you, but there are definite signals that a spouse who cares will never ignore.

Pay attention to your spouse in public without being overly demonstrative. Let others know you love each other. Designing people rarely move in unless they sense there is a chance for success. Let them know there is nothing they can cling to, that you and your spouse love each other and intend to be faithful to each other and to the Lord.

Watch out for the perpetual counselees who must see you after every service. Suggest that your spouse join you for counseling sessions. If the counselee refuses, you've discovered the truth. In fact, your spouse may detect the danger before you do. It is unwise to counsel a member of the opposite sex when you're alone. Your church office should be adjacent to that of a secretary or an assistant, if possible. If you must go to the counselee's home, take your spouse along. If the counselee insists on absolute privacy, arrange for it in a place where there is high visibility and some people who can see you even if they can't hear the conversation.

Don't permit people in the church to form a fan club. It is difficult to have a spiritual ministry among people who see you as a substitute husband, boyfriend, wife, or girlfriend. By accepting their applause, you're doing them very little good and they're doing you a great deal of harm. First Timothy 5:1–3 suggests that we treat the members of the church as we do the members of our own family. This is wise counsel.

Pastors don't have to commit immoral acts to ruin their testimony and ministry. Suspicion and gossip will do the job. "Keep yourself pure" (1 Tim. 5:22). One pastor warned his handsome assistant about designing women, and the assistant said, "But there's safety in numbers." "Yes," said the pastor, "but there's more safety in exodus!" Joseph would have agreed with that advice.

We repeat: if your own marriage is all it ought to be, and your walk with God is a good one, you should have few problems along this line. A chaste mind helps to maintain a chaste life. At the start of every day, give God your body as a living sacrifice and spend time in the Word to renew your mind (Rom. 12:1–2). Watch and pray, "because the one who is in you is greater than the one who is in the world" (1 John 4:4).

Chapter SEVENTEEN

Personal Matters

---

*How should I budget my time so I can
get more done each day?*

Budget isn't the correct word—the word is *prioritize*. To budget means to set aside specific amounts of time for definite tasks; to prioritize means to arrange your tasks in order of importance and use your best time for your most essential tasks. Suppose you budget thirty hours a week for study but end up with only twenty? Then what?

Generally speaking, a pastor's priorities are: (1) God, (2) home, (3) the weekly preaching, (4) pastoral work, (5) administration, and (6) whatever's left over. An efficient day begins with an effective quiet time before the day begins. Unless you begin your day in the Word and prayer, committing yourself and your work to God, you'll not make the best use of your time. Jesus arose early in the morning to pray (Mark 1:35; and see Isa. 50:4–5), and certainly we can't do less. It was John Henry Jowett (*The Preacher: His Life and Work*, Hodderah and Stoughton, London, 116) who said that he had to be at his desk working when he heard the workmen's boots sounding on the street, for how could the servant of God lie in bed while the members of his flock were already at work?

Use your mornings for study and be in your study at the same hour each day. Don't make a public announcement that you want to be left alone unless you have the kind of rapport with your people that can stand a strain. Their attitude is (right or wrong): "We pay his salary, and he should be available." It takes time, but gradually educate your people not to phone or stop in ("I was in the neighborhood ...") when you're preparing their spiritual meals. A word in the ears of your best officers may help get the message out.

Devote your afternoons to visiting, mail, phone calls, and church administration. Make all your necessary phone calls at one time and they'll go faster. When you read your mail, jot replies in the margins and you won't have to read the letters again when you reply. Try to set up counseling appointments for afternoons. No doubt your evenings will be given to committee work, special visitation, and those all-important times at home with your family.

Learn to say no to most outside invitations, especially during your first year or two at a church. Pastors do need to minister to others outside their flocks, but not to the neglect of their own ministries. Add new responsibilities and ministries gradually, and never take on a new ministry until you feel at home with the ones you already have. Too many men feel they must set the world on fire their first month on the field. They start publishing a paper, they begin a daily radio program, and they feel obligated to speak at every meeting in town. Their branches go out farther than their roots go deep, and eventually the tree falls over. There's nothing wrong with church publications, radio programs, or speaking at other meetings; but these things must come in their time.

Carry a pocket notebook or a personal digital assistant (PDA) and use it. Don't trust your memory and don't write notes on little pieces of paper that can easily be lost. Carry the kind of equipment that enables you to keep track of appointments, jobs to be done, expenses, and special notes. Use it! Arrange a schedule for the day, the week, and the month. Each evening, check off the jobs completed and make a new list for the next day. All of this sounds elementary, but it works. "You plan your work and you work your plan." This is the program followed by the masters of industry, men and women who get things done.

At least once a year, make a list of everything you're doing and see how many of these jobs can better be done by others. This is delegating. There's no reason why the pastor has to run the photocopier, fold the bulletins, lick the stamps, and mend the hymnals. Find people in the church who can do these jobs for you. After all, the pastor's task is to help the members do "the work of the ministry" (Eph. 4:11–12 KJV).

There will be days when your schedule will fall apart, but you need not fall apart with it. Trust God to help you get your work done. Stick to your priorities. Your church will rise or fall on the strength of your pulpit ministry and your pastoral work.

Take a day off each week, and take your allotted vacation. "But the Devil doesn't take a day off!" someone may lament. True, but the Devil doesn't have a physical body, and Satan is hardly our example in the ministry. Jesus knew that his disciples needed a time of rest (Mark 6:30–32), and he knows that we need rest, too. Pick the day that best suits you and your church schedule. Monday is not always the best day, because you often learn things on Sunday that ought to be taken care of immediately, and there goes your day off. Thursday is a good day for a break, especially after working up to a midweek service. And don't overdo it on Saturdays. Many prominent preachers of the past would not be out on a Saturday evening, but would spend that time preparing their own souls for the Lord's Day and praying for their people.

Never waste those extra minutes that come your way. If you're going to the barbershop or the doctor's office, take a book along and avoid wasting time reading old magazines. As suggested in chapter 6, you should plan to relax a bit before and after your evening meal and you can use some of that time to read. However, don't ignore your family, especially your spouse who may have things to talk about. A relaxing evening is also a good time to work your way quickly through the periodicals that arrive at your home or office, mark items to file, etc.

During the day, if you find yourself getting nervous and tense, stop to pray and turn everything over to God. The Holy Spirit is infinitely efficient; he alone can lubricate the machinery of your life. It's when we trust in our own strength and wisdom that we go on time-wasting detours. "Let the peace of Christ rule [be umpire] in your hearts" (Col. 3:15).

Most of us resent interruptions, but sometimes they bring us opportunities for ministry. Keep margins in your life and the interruptions won't upset things that much. Often the interruptions turn out to be the ministry.

HOW CAN I MAINTAIN A BURDEN FOR SOULS, AND HOW CAN I COMMUNICATE THIS BURDEN TO MY PEOPLE?

As with visitation, soul winning is better caught than taught. If the pastor has a burden for souls, it will show in every aspect of the ministry—preaching, teaching, administration, counseling, weddings, funerals. Soul winning isn't something we turn on and off like the radio. It's the central concern of our lives as we seek to glorify Christ.

We maintain our burden for souls by doing our job. The more we share Christ with others, the brighter the fire burns. When we feel our hearts getting cold, we must pray for the Spirit's fullness and then go out to talk to somebody about Jesus. We must ask God to make real to us what it means for a soul to be lost and without hope. (Jonah had that experience—Jonah 4.) If we're in daily fellowship with Christ, our hearts will be kept warm and tender and we will want to share Him with others.

Read books about evangelism and effective soul winners. You can't read a life of D. L. Moody, Billy Sunday, or Gipsy Smith without your own heart being moved. This doesn't mean we serve with borrowed fire, but it does mean we get inspiration from their lives. Soul winners now in heaven can provoke us to good works!

Have a list of lost people you know and use it for regular prayer and visitation. When you meet with your officers for prayer, share the names of the unsaved. As these people come to Christ, it will bring great joy to your heart and to the hearts of your leaders.

Nothing fans the sparks of zeal like the joy of seeing people trust the Savior.

WHAT SHOULD I DO WHEN I HIT ONE OF THOSE DISCOURAGING DAYS IN MY MINISTRY?

The first step toward overcoming discouragement is to realize that these experiences come to everybody. All the books on "the deeper life" notwithstanding, you will have days of discouragement and depression. Moses had them; so did Elijah, David, and Paul. (Have you read 2 Corinthians 1 lately?) Don't feel you have lost your calling or sinned away God's blessing just because you have a cloudy day.

When that day comes, face it honestly. Above all, make no important decisions. Many faithful servants have hurt their ministries by foolishly resigning out of the will of God, simply because on a dark day they felt like failures. Talk over your feelings with a close friend, and pray for God's grace. Spend some time with your wife and children. Get out and get ventilated. Sometimes the basic cause is physical: what you need is fresh air, exercise, and a change of pace. (Remember Elijah? What he needed was a good nap!) When you feel one of these dark days about to hit you, make your plans accordingly.

Be patient with yourself and with the Lord. "This too shall pass." It's amazing how different the situation will look twenty-four hours later. Watch out for self-pity: this is the poison that kills the joy of ministry. Also, beware of getting critical of your people. In the darkness, everything looks out of proportion, so wait for the sun to shine. When God gives you light, you'll see that most of the things you feared were really only shadows.

In many cases, simply committing yourself to God and going out to minister to somebody else will hasten your recovery. There's no therapy more potent than encouraging another child of God. If you sit at home sulking, or sit in your study licking your wounds, you'll only get worse. Do something active. Before long, the old faith and joy will come back.

Pastors who suffer from chronic discouragement, even to the point of despair, should secure professional counsel.

How often should I minister away from my own field?

The first year or so you are on a field, stay close to home. You need to be in the pulpit, feeding the flock, and giving them opportunity to get to know you. After that, you can think about a wider ministry, but let the Lord open the doors.

If you're sensible in your planning and you put your church first, your people will let you make your own schedule and won't complain. If you're away too much, you'll only hurt yourself and the church. If you find yourself wanting to be gone, perhaps it is time you consider a change. A spiritual father loves his children in the Lord and wants to be with them. The sheep need a faithful shepherd, not a kangaroo who hops in and out of the pasture. While you're on the field, if you faithfully minister to the people, they will not begrudge you opportunities to minister in other places. In fact, they will be proud that others want to hear their pastor.

Of course, a church needs to be taught that the pastor's wider ministry is good both for the pastor and for them. It's good for the pastor to occasionally have a change of location and pace and to be a blessing to others. It's been our experience that the wider ministry is more difficult than staying at home, but we invariably returned home eager to minister to our people and having learned something new and fresh while away. It is good for the church when the pastor is away occasionally. They get to hear other preachers, and they get a blessing by sharing their pastor with others. After all, the pastor is a gift to the whole church as well as to one local church (Eph. 4:8–15).

Except for the annual vacation, or other special occasions, the pastor shouldn't be away two Sundays in a row. If you find yourself a stranger in your own pulpit, you've been gone too often. If you detect that the sheep are restless, then you had better stay home. Some churches have a set number of weeks for the pastor to use for outside meetings. If so, abide by the policy and don't complain. If God wants to give you a wider ministry, he will also give opportunity for making necessary changes in the policy. Just be sure that, when you go elsewhere to preach, you do so because you want to be a blessing and not because you want to escape the problems in your own church.

Finally, keep a close watch on the total church calendar, and don't be away at important times of the year. Your church is your base of ministry, not your sphere of ministry, but don't undermine the base. If you do, you may find you have no ministry at all.

I'M EMBARRASSED TO ASK THIS, BUT HOW DO YOU GO ABOUT LETTING THE CHURCH KNOW YOU NEED A RAISE? IS IT UNSPIRITUAL TO DISCUSS FINANCES?

No need to be embarrassed! How a church handles its money and cares for its staff and its missionaries is a very spiritual matter. Most churches have a policy of reviewing salaries annually. A pastor ought to get at least a cost-of-living increase and, if the work of the church is prospering, a merit increase (1 Tim. 5:17–18). Before you accept a call, discuss this matter with the board and find out what their policy is. You owe it to them (and to your family) to be open and direct without seeming to be grasping.

One thing you must never do is bring your personal finances into the pulpit, or drop hints here and there in the church. Your spouse should also be careful not to discuss money with people in the church. Talk to God about your needs, and be patient. If the church is insensitive to your needs, God will meet the needs some other way, but the church will be the loser. It is unfortunate that some churches try to get bargains when they call a pastor and then wonder why God never seems to bless them. The church that takes care of its pastor will discover that God will take care of the church.

There's always a need for stewardship education in a church. If you're preaching the Word faithfully, you will have to deal with God's views about wealth and giving, so don't skirt the issue. We're commanded to tell people how God wants them to use the wealth he places in their hands (1 Tim. 6:17–19).

If you want to become rich, the ministry is not the place to go. It's been our experience that God meets every need and gives us above and beyond what we deserve. Any sacrifices we make are more than compensated for in other ways by our gracious Father. Don't become obsessed with money. Matthew 6:33 should be our guide.

How can I make my devotional life more meaningful?

Pastors handle the spiritual treasures of the Word day after day, and if they're not careful, they will lose "the wonder of it all." You make four or five visits and pray in each home or hospital room, and you may find yourself praying rather routinely. Even daily study of the Word can become routine. Phillips Brooks in his *Lectures on Preaching* rightly said, "Familiarity does not breed contempt except of contemptible things or in contemptible people." The problem doesn't lie with the Word or with prayer, but with the minister's own heart.

We need uninterrupted time to meditate on the Word and pray. Start each day with a definite meeting with God. Once you begin to measure this meeting on the clock, you'll start to put out the fire. No matter how busy we think we are, we must never permit the morning watch to be neglected or a hasty routine.

Many pastors find it helpful to use different translations for their devotional Bible reading, always seeking to hear the voice of the Lord. We can become so familiar with our favorite version that it no longer speaks to us. A wide-margin edition is helpful because you can write notes as God speaks to you; but be careful that your devotional time doesn't become a time for sermon preparation. We're there to meet with God and to hear him speak to us personally—to *our* needs—and if he meets our needs, he will work through us to meet the needs of others. If you've ever tried to breathe in once and breathe out twice, you know that you can't give out unless you take it in.

Use a notebook for a devotional diary and write down the truths God gives you as you meditate. Have separate pages for prayer requests for each day of the week and one page for those special things we pray about daily. If we pray about the same things every day, our prayers can become perfunctory. Let the Spirit guide you, not the notebook page.

If we're ministering to our people as we ought, there will be sufficient burdens on our hearts to make us want to pray for them. God has a way of putting us into the furnace when we need it! The closer you come to the needs of people, the less sufficient you will feel, and the more you will have to turn to God for help. "And who is equal to such a task?" asks Paul, and then he answers his question, "Our competence comes from God" (2 Cor. 2:16; 3:5).

Read the great devotional classics, but not as a substitute for your Bible. Reading a published sermon occasionally just to feed your own soul is an excellent spiritual exercise. Remember, the pastor often doesn't get to hear others preach, and our own soul can be starved for a sermon. Don't always read sermons by the same preachers, no matter how much you enjoy them; vary the spiritual diet.

It's a good practice to meet regularly with a fellow pastor for prayer. Fortunate is the pastor who has a praying friend. Be honest with each other: it will do you both good.

Our spiritual life starts to deteriorate when we start praying things we don't mean, preaching things that we don't practice, and expecting things of others that we don't do ourselves. It's important that we take time to examine our own hearts for any signs of erosion. We must apply the Word to our own lives before we dare apply it to the lives of others.

No doubt you will discover certain parts of the Bible, and certain devotional books, that will just hit the spot when battle fatigue sets in. Get away from home or church for an hour or two, and let God clean the old ashes from the altar of your soul.

You cannot separate the inner life from the outer life. One of the best ways to stir up the flame of devotion is to go out to minister to somebody in need. "Give, and it will be given to you" (Luke 6:38). A self-centered devotional life is not a Christ-centered one. We receive the living water that we might be channels to share the blessing with others (John 7:37–39).

WHERE CAN I TAKE MY TROUBLES AND FIND HELP AND ENCOURAGEMENT? I PRAY A LOT AND TALK THINGS OVER AT HOME, BUT I WISH I COULD "UNLOAD" ON SOME SAINTLY APOSTLE OR PROPHET.

The loneliness of leadership is one of the most difficult things to bear. If you read biographies at all, you know how true this is.

Psalm 23:1 can be translated, "The Lord is my pastor." We believe that God wants to pastor his servants and that he's able to take us through the difficult places of life. Certainly there is special grace for the minister who preaches the Word and shepherds the flock. The Lord will not desert us!

But it's also good to have someone to share our burdens with, and this is where an older, more experienced pastor comes in. Fortunate is that younger preacher who has a mature pastor-friend who will patiently listen to ministry problems! Usually in every area there are godly and experienced ministers whose doors and hearts are open to younger servants. Even a telephone conversation over the miles can help lift the burden.

Sometimes you will find a godly couple in the church whose hearts seem bound to your heart, and you can feel free to talk with them. It is unwise to open your heart to just anybody in the church, but the young pastor can share his burdens with some mature couple (or perhaps an older officer) and not have to worry about the consequences.

Above all else, beware of self-pity. Self-pity is the first step toward defeat in the ministry because it nourishes our pride. Loneliness and self-pity often travel together. If you find self-pity invading your heart, get out and do something for somebody else or just enjoy some exercise—play golf, go for a walk, go window-shopping—but do something! It's our experience that discouragement sometimes is a symptom of physical weariness, and perhaps the best thing you can do is take a nap.

DOES THE LORD EVER LEAD US TO RESIGN WHEN WE DON'T HAVE ANOTHER PLACE TO GO?

Not usually, but it does happen. We find few, if any, people in the Bible standing around waiting for God to direct them. One task is usually preparation for the next. In fact, not having a church could be a serious barrier to getting a call from another church. Most pulpit committees are looking for a pastor who's busy in a church and doing something.

It's been our experience that God begins to stir the heart long before he moves the body. If you're walking with the Lord, he'll direct you and his timing will never be off. Many pastors resign in haste and repent in leisure. Had they only waited a few months, the tide would have turned and the work would have prospered. V. Raymond Edman, for many years president of Wheaton College (Illinois), often reminded the students, "It's always too soon to quit."

The lives of Bible leaders, and the lives of historic leaders of the church, all seem to indicate that God works patiently, according to a definite plan. God rarely keeps a faithful worker waiting and wondering, unless there is some lesson to learn that can't be learned any other way.

The difference between a true shepherd and a hireling is that the hireling runs away when the going gets tough (John 10:1–14). Faithful pastors never leave a ministry; they go to a ministry because the Lord has called them there. There is a difference.

NOTES

REFLECTIONS

ACTION POINTS

Chapter EIGHTEEN

The Pastor and His Priorities

*What are the basic priorities in
Christian ministry?*

We've mentioned this before but it won't hurt to review and maybe go a little deeper. We suggest that your priorities look like this:

◆ 1. Your personal devotional life. Everything you do rises or falls on your faithfulness here. "Apart from me you can do nothing" (John 15:5).

◆ 2. Your family's faith. Your ministry begins at home. Another person can pastor the church, but only you can be spouse and parent in your home.

◆ 3. A burden for souls. Keep the fire burning; otherwise your ministry will become cold and academic.

◆ 4. Study. Don't settle for secondhand sermons. Do your own work and dig for the spiritual treasures. Guard your morning hours and invest them in concentrated study.

◆ 5. Preaching. History reveals that the spiritual level of churches rises or falls depending on the faithful preaching of the Word. Don't allow the pressure of the immediate to steal the time you need for sermon preparation. Learn to say no and control that daily schedule.

6. Pastoral ministry. This personal contact with your people will help balance the work for you. The preacher must be a pastor if the Word is to touch lives in a personal way. The people you help will help you. We learn by taking in but we grow by giving out.

7. The day-by-day administrative work of the church. Since the shepherd is a leader, this is also pastoral work, so don't minimize it or ignore it. However, don't get involved in the numerous details of the church's ministry. The ministerial micromanager will end up delivering sermonettes and developing Christianettes. It takes time to be holy—and to help others grow in holiness.

We don't look at priorities as rungs on a ladder, but rather as spokes in a wheel. The hub of the wheel is your walk with God: everything else comes out from that. Paul did many things, but they were all controlled by that decisive "one thing I do" (Phil. 3:13).

HOW DOES ONE MEASURE SUCCESS IN MINISTRY?

It's odd but true that many of the successful pastors in history believed they were failures. Perhaps it's because a growing minister is never satisfied and wants to see the Lord do more. God rarely allows his servants to see all the good they're doing.

If the pastor is growing personally, then the church will grow. If there's a sameness and tameness about your life, watch out. If there is no excitement in the study of the Word and the preparing of messages, if pastoral work is boring, if you find yourself arriving at the office late and leaving early, if you start being defensive, then spiritual erosion has set in and both you and your church will suffer. If the work is a challenge, and if you eagerly anticipate ministering the Word publicly and from house to house, then it's likely that God is blessing and the work is growing.

There is a book in the Bible called Numbers—but numbers alone are not everything. Where there's life, there's growth. Charles Spurgeon used to say that the only people who criticized statistics were those who had none to report. Perhaps he was right. The Holy Spirit counted numbers in the book of Acts, but the numbers were the results of the ministry of dedicated men and women. We want our churches to grow, not so that we can count people, but because people count. Sometimes there's a slow, steady growth; at other times, God gives a rich harvest. But numerical increase is one indication that God is at work, provided the increase is not the result of man-made, carnal gimmicks.

Increase in offerings is also a test of spiritual success. If the sheep are fed, they will give. When they're starving, they start biting each other. When the ministry is being blessed of God, there's an atmosphere of love, confidence, and service in the church. For the most part, the people will love each other and seek to minister to each other. You'll always have problems to solve and battles to fight, because a church is made up of people; but these problems won't grow into crises. The ability of a church to face and solve problems is an indication of spiritual growth. Also, the appearance of new problems indicates that the church is on the move. Never be afraid of disagreements in the church: where there is movement, there may be friction. The lack of friction may mean the church is no longer on the move.

If you've set definite goals for your ministry, achieving these goals one by one will be an indication that you are making progress. The pastor who simply drifts from week to week will always be discouraged, because he doesn't know where he is going. "When the pilot doesn't know what port he's heading for, no wind is the right wind."

Second Corinthians 10:7–13 is a clear warning against the wrong kind of self-evaluation. It's easy for a church to become a mutual-admiration society. The true measure of a church's ministry isn't what it's doing as compared to some other church (which may be smaller), but what it's doing as compared with its own potential. The church that could have a thousand in Sunday school, but rests content with two hundred, is failing.

Never forget that churches go through stages of growth, not unlike that of the human body. The infancy of a new church is exciting, not unlike the birth of a baby. But then things settle down, and you reach childhood, when the church must be taught and trained. In adolescence your people seem to manufacture problems. Once you reach spiritual maturity, keep at it. Be sure that the church is winning souls so that new life is steadily coming into the body. Once a church gets into spiritual old age, you will have serious problems: the next step is "second childhood" (see Heb. 5:12)! It is a wise pastor who senses the times and the seasons, and who preaches and plans accordingly.

As we said before, the Lord rarely lets his servants see how much good they're doing. When you feel the most discouraged, God is probably using you in the greatest way. Be faithful (1 Cor. 4:2). God will take care of the rest. The soldiers in the trenches don't see the progress of the entire battle, but the general knows what he's doing. Do your work faithfully and leave the results with the Lord.

Read 1 Corinthians 3 and note the three pictures of the church: a family (vv. 1–4), the field (vv. 5–9), and the temple (vv. 10–22). The goal of the family is maturity, the goal of the field is quantity, and the goal of the temple is quality. When you see your people maturing and becoming more like Jesus, the family is succeeding. If they are laboring and seeing a harvest, the church is succeeding. If you and your leaders are carefully using the Word and wisdom of God to build the church, then you are experiencing success. Don't measure yourself by some popular high-profile pastor or your church by their churches, because each situation is unique and no two churches are alike. The command "work out your salvation with fear and trembling" (Phil. 2:12) is in the plural—Paul was addressing the whole congregation. God has a special plan for each church and it's our privilege to find what that plan is and follow it.

Chapter NINETEEN

The Ministry of the Pastor's Wife

Note: Realizing that women as well as men serve in Christian ministry, we've kept the previous chapters gender neutral. But we felt the pastor's wife has some unique situations and problems that deserve special attention. Most of the material in this chapter was provided by Lucile Sugden and Betty Wiersbe.

How important is the pastor's wife to the work of the ministry?

She's very important! Her attitude helps to set the tone of the home, and this affects her husband and family and therefore touches the ministry at the church. If your wife is a capable manager at home (keeping the books, paying the bills, etc.), it will give you more time for ministry. Fortunate is the pastor whose wife knows how to oversee the activities of the family. While the pastor's wife is not an assistant pastor—if she is, she certainly doesn't collect a salary!—her love for Christ and his people will have an impact on the church family. If she's a bad example as a believer, a wife, or a mother, there will be painful consequences that can only hurt the ministry. Whether she feels like it or not, she's the "first lady" of the church and the other women will either admire her or criticize her, or perhaps do both. She lives in a glass house, and that isn't easy; but it's a great opportunity to influence others for the Lord.

MUST THE PASTOR'S WIFE HAVE A SPECIAL CALL TO MINISTRY?

It's certainly a great asset if she knows God has called her into his service and that she and her husband are laborers together. The demands of the ministry are great, and it helps when the minister's wife is confident she's right where God wants her. This means pulling together, praying together, working together, hurting together, and trusting together. If she decides to go in another direction, or if her interests are divided, that can only create problems both in the home and in the church.

A confident call from the Lord makes for unity as you serve together. Yes, there are sacrifices for her to make—interrupted schedules, evening meetings, late-night emergencies—but it's all part of the calling. So is the extra entertaining she'll have to do. We feel sorry for the minister whose wife has her own agenda and talks about "your work" and "my work."

WHAT'S THE MOST IMPORTANT MINISTRY OF THE PASTOR'S WIFE?

Being a godly woman and using her gifts and abilities to serve the Lord, first at home and then at the church. Husband and wife must work together to make the home a place of refuge and joy, to the glory of God. However, regardless of a person's vocation, building a strong Christian home demands hard work and sacrifice, prayer and patience, but when you're in the ministry, you face some special challenges. The husband must make it clear to the search committee that his wife will serve loyally at his side, but that the church isn't calling her as an unpaid assistant. If there are small children in the home, they need her loving care. You must protect and defend your wife and deliver her from people who would like to run her life.

HOW CAN I HELP MY WIFE FULFILL HER RESPONSIBILITIES?

By praying for her faithfully and being sensitive to her needs. You and your wife must pray together every day, morning and evening, as well as have your own private devotional times; and you must pray with your children also. You should know what her schedule is and try to help when you can. By all means keep her informed of your schedule and be sure to tell her when there are changes, especially if those changes affect meals or activities with the children. When you get called away on an emergency, phone her so she can anticipate any delays that might affect family plans.

Make arrangements for your wife to have time away from home, even if it's only to browse through the shopping mall or have lunch with a friend. If you have small children, bring your study books home occasionally and relieve your wife, and don't feel guilty about it! Remember, the best thing you can do for your church is to build a happy Christian home. If your wife has a hobby—and she should, if only to "switch gears" occasionally—enter into her interests and encourage her.

HOW SHOULD MY WIFE HANDLE CRITICISM ABOUT ME AND HERSELF?

No matter how much honest criticism may help us, unkind criticism hurts, and it isn't easy to handle. People in ministry have to expect criticism because it goes with the work of leadership. If people don't like the preacher, they'll criticize his wife and children. Most criticism can be overlooked and even laughed at, but some of it is born in the pit of hell (James 3:6) and has to be silenced.

Criticism that doesn't hurt you may hurt your wife, so don't treat it lightly. That will only make her hurt even more. Take her feelings seriously, listen compassionately, and then pray together. We must learn to forgive those who spitefully use us and leave the matter with the Lord. It takes time for a stabbed heart to heal, but the Lord can "bind up the brokenhearted" (Isa. 61:1).

After you've been in the church awhile, you'll probably discover who the gossips and critics are and be able to lovingly confront them. But don't get detoured from your main work—building a godly home and a godly church.

SHOULD A PASTOR'S WIFE WORK OUTSIDE THE HOME?

Years ago, the answer would have been a resounding "No!" Most churches expected the pastor's wife to devote herself twenty-four hours a day to the church and her home, in that order. But times have changed and so have the economics of raising a family. Unless the church is very generous, many ministerial homes today need two incomes in order to provide the basics of life plus insurance, education, transportation, and the many things that balanced families seem to need these days.

Furthermore, if your wife has special training—nursing or teaching, for example—why should she lose her hard-earned credentials by abandoning her vocation? Many other wives in the church work outside their homes, so why not the pastor's wife? In smaller communities, your wife can have a Christian influence in the marketplace, and most of the people she meets would applaud her for what she's doing. In larger communities, nobody knows the difference. The decision lies with you and your wife, not you and the church board. However, discuss it with the search committee before you accept a call.

Most churches today are much more flexible about working wives than they were years ago, but church approval is no guarantee of heaven's blessing. You and your wife must weigh the matter, pray, and make sure you know God's will. We've seen more than one ministerial marriage end in divorce because the husband and wife were marching to different drummers. No matter how much money they made, it just wasn't worth it.

WHAT IF MY WIFE AND I DISAGREE ABOUT MINISTRY DECISIONS AND PLANS FOR THE CHURCH?

Wise is the pastor who listens to his godly wife! Many times there's more sense in a woman's so-called intuition than in some of the training you received in seminary or at the last seminar you attended. Your wife must never command a course of action in the ministry, and she should stand with you even if she disagrees; but at the same time, you must give her the right to exercise her spiritual gifts and share her concerns with you. If she's spiritually minded, she will pray much before telling you why she disagrees with you, and she'll listen to what you have to say. You and your wife must be united in the important decisions of life. If the Enemy can divide you, he's well on his way to a great victory in your home and in your ministry.

We know of one wife who publicly disagreed with her husband in church business meetings. She may have had some good counsel to offer him, but she was tactless in giving it publicly when she could have his undivided attention at home. The ministry didn't last long.

WHAT MINISTRIES SHOULD THE PASTOR'S WIFE HAVE IN THE CHURCH?

Her gifts and talents will determine this, and not all ministry wives are alike. We don't think she should hold an elected office in the church, except perhaps in the women's organization. Better that she train other women. She can always encourage and help from the sidelines and let other people take the credit.

But if your wife has special gifts, in music or teaching, for example, don't let her bury her talent just because she married a pastor. Be sure that nobody gets the idea that you both are "taking over the church." If the two of you have too many jobs in the church, then what will happen if God moves you elsewhere? It's fine to fill some of the gaps temporarily, but don't let your wife sacrifice herself and her family because others refuse to serve and prefer to watch her work.

If she has a gift of teaching, she must use it; but even if she doesn't, encourage your wife to be a good Bible student. This will help her as a believer, a wife, a mother, and a counselor. In some churches, the pastor and his wife team-teach a mixed class. Sometimes they teach a class for new Christians or for newlyweds. Wait on the Lord and he'll find her the right niche. There are ways for her to serve in areas for which she is best suited, and her service need not create problems.

SHOULD I SHARE WITH MY WIFE CONFIDENTIAL INFORMATION ABOUT PEOPLE AND PROBLEMS IN THE CHURCH?

Generally speaking, no. You protect each other from the snooping gossips when you can both honestly say, "My husband [my wife] has said nothing to me about that." In time, the amateur investigative reporters in the church will stop interrogating you. You and your wife need to talk and pray together about church problems. You may discover that what you thought was a confidential matter is actually something your children heard in a youth meeting weeks ago and reported to their mother. You need your wife's insight and prayer support, and it does you good to talk problems over with her. Often she can lovingly help to give you a balanced perspective on the problem, and that will make it easier for you to minister to the people involved.

But the other side of the coin is this: when your wife is told something confidential, and she sees that you are moving in the wrong direction and likely to make the problem worse, what should she do? Here is where you and your wife must trust each other. When she says, "My dear, I wouldn't do that if I were you," you need to listen and not ask questions. She may want to phone her confidant and say, "I believe the time has come for my husband to know what you have told me. May I have your permission to share it with him?" If the answer is no, then she must commit it to the Lord and help you all she can without breaking confidence.

When somebody shares a matter with you or your wife and asks that it be kept confidential, each of you should feel free to say: "My wife [husband] and I share the burdens of the ministry together. If at some time in the future I feel she [he] should know about this, do I have your permission to tell her [him]? I assure you that I won't do it unless I feel it's absolutely necessary." Most people will say, "Yes, I'll trust you to do what's right."

Confidentiality is important to the ministry. Your people must have faith in your word or they may not have faith in your preaching and teaching. Whenever you're tempted to talk to somebody about a matter entrusted to your care, talk to the Lord about it instead.

How can I help my wife have a happy ministry both in the home and in the church?

The same way any Christian husband can make his wife happy: by fulfilling the marriage vows and living for the Lord. If you pray for your wife, love her, and seek in every way to make her happy, and she reciprocates, then your home will be a heaven on earth.

But as a minister, you must pay attention to some special things. For instance, don't use your wife and family as sermon illustrations unless they say it's okay. Even if the story is funny and makes you the butt of the joke, don't tell it without their permission. Your wife and children already live in the glare of the spotlights, so please don't drag them into the sermons against their will. It's tough enough to be a pastor's kid without having to endure that kind of punishment.

Encourage your wife to cultivate meaningful friendships with other women in the area, especially other ministry wives. If it seems unwise for her to build close friendships within the church family, she must look elsewhere for the feminine companionship that every woman needs.

Ask God to give you an older couple in the church who will move into your home and care for your children while your wife goes with you on trips. She needs to get away, and you need to have her with you. In these days of multiplied ministerial scandals, your church board will approve of your wife accompanying you when you minister out of town.

Encourage your wife to be herself and not an imitation of somebody else, especially the wife of the former pastor. ("My, she was such a gifted speaker!") Compliment her, encourage her to develop her skills, give her room to grow, and together you will "serve the Lord with gladness."

One final word of counsel: if you're frustrated or angry, don't take it out on your wife and family. When you arrive home for the evening meal, make everybody in the home happy that you're there. Discipline yourself to enjoy your home and family first, and then later in the evening you and your wife can chat and pray about the burdens and hurts of the day. (Don't forget that she has her share of hurts and burdens, too, and so do the children.) God forbid that your children should look out the window and shout, "Look out! Daddy's home!"

WHAT SHOULD WE DO WHEN WE START TO HAVE
SERIOUS PROBLEMS AT HOME?

It's our conviction that the heart of every problem is the problem in the heart, so begin by searching your own hearts and seeking God's cleansing and forgiveness. If both of you are honest with God and with each other, and are willing to apologize and to forgive, then God can begin to bring about healing. This must be the first step.

However, some problems may have longer, deeper roots than you imagined, and once you start to work on them, new problems start developing. Seek a competent Christian counselor who can help you spiritually and emotionally. It's a humbling experience for a pastor and his wife to meet with a counselor, but it can also be an experience of healing and maturing.

If the problem involves one of your children, this is especially painful. If you share the burden with the church family, your child may be embarrassed and hurt, but if you don't share it and the news comes out gradually, your integrity may be damaged. It's usually best to tell the official family and ask them to make it a matter of prayer. The word may gradually "trickle down" to the congregation. Your adversaries in the church may use the problem as ammunition to attack you, but most of the people will stand with you and show you special love and concern. After all, they've had family problems, too.

You'll be amazed at what God will do in you and for you as you and the church share the burden. God can give you new tenderness and love that will deeply affect your pastoral work and your preaching. You will discover that others in the church have gone through the same valley, and they will minister to you.

Since we're all human, we in the ministry have to be vulnerable. Who are we that we should be exempt from Satan's attacks or life's burdens? Martin Luther said that "prayer, meditation, and temptation made a minister," and he was right. Our trials drive us to the Word of God and prayer, and this can only make us better Christians and better servants. Like Jesus Christ our Lord, we must be wounded healers.

Chapter TWENTY

Miscellaneous Ministerial Matters

*What do you think is the greatest need
in churches today?*

In one word, revival, which simply means replacing pretense with reality. The church is so much like the world that we don't seem to have much influence on the world, and only the Holy Spirit can change this. We've substituted promotion for prayer and entertainment for worship and preaching, and we fear that much of our so-called "success" may be shallow and temporary. What was once a sanctuary is today more like a theater, and the glory has departed.

God usually begins with his servants. We thank God for reports that, here and there, pastors are meeting together for prayer and are replacing walls with bridges. Until God's people get right with the Lord and each other, revival will not come. The church that decides to get back to basics—the Word of God and prayer—can experience God's blessing.

Perhaps in your pastoral prayer each Sunday, you could ask God to send revival. While you're at it, ask him to bless some other church in your community. If pastors and churches start praying for one another publicly each Lord's Day, the Spirit might begin to work among them.

While it's true that spiritual awakening is a sovereign act of God, it's also true that the promise of 2 Chronicles 7:14 is still in God's Word.

A PROFESSIONALISM SEEMS TO BE DEVELOPING IN THE MINISTRY TODAY. PASTORS ARE NO LONGER SHEPHERDS OR SERVANTS; THEY'RE MORE LIKE CEOS. HOW DO YOU VIEW THIS?

With alarm. Only God knows what's going on in the hearts of his servants, but we do see some trends that disturb us. For one thing, the local church is now viewed as a corporation with the pastor as the CEO, the deacons/elders as the corporate board, and numbers as the major measure of success. The philosophy seems to be, "If it works for IBM, it will work for the church."

But God doesn't always think and act the way we do in our successful corporate structures (Isa. 55:8–9). There are dozens of images of the church in the New Testament, but the corporation isn't among them. Yes, the church must be businesslike in its operation, but the church is not a business. We can learn from the experts, but we must be careful to test everything by the Word of God. When the pastor ceases to be a shepherd, what will happen to the sheep? (See Ezek. 34.) When a church is run like a business, will nonmeasurable things (like the fruit of the Spirit) really count?

Every church wants to experience growth, but true growth comes from nutrition and not merely addition. We should organize for efficiency, but we must also agonize for God's sufficiency; otherwise, what we think are blessings may turn out to be curses. The church doesn't need to imitate the world in order to experience the blessing of heaven. Campbell Morgan said, "The church did the most for the world when the church was the least like the world."

WHAT'S THE BEST WAY TO MINISTER TO RETIREES IN THE CHURCH?

Senior citizens represent a large segment of today's population in America and are a great labor force for us to enlist and a mission field for us to harvest. The senior saints in our churches ought to be trained and challenged to serve. Every church should have a seniors' ministry that mobilizes and motivates retirees to live for Christ and serve him.

Too often a seniors' ministry is mostly fun and games, food and fellowship, and lots of trips, and their spiritual needs are either ignored or given only token acknowledgment. This is a mistake. There's certainly nothing wrong with a group of people enjoying a bus trip or a dinner, but the Christian life is more than enjoyment. There's also the matter of enlistment in the service of the Lord and the enrichment of their own lives.

Retirees have more discretionary time and money than any other population segment, and these days and dollars ought to be captured for the Lord. These people are often the prayer warriors in the church, and we dare not give them the impression that they can now take a vacation. "I've done my share in the church," they sometimes say, "so now it's time for somebody else to do the work." They retire not only from their jobs, but also from the Christian life!

Your seniors' ministry must have a definite statement of purpose that includes involvement as well as enjoyment. They need to learn about home and foreign missions, because God sometimes calls retirees to serve on the mission field. They should be taught how to witness and lead the lost to Christ. There are incredible opportunities for ministry all over your community if only you will look for them. Whoever pastors the seniors must have a heart for older folks and believe that they have a great contribution to make to the Lord's work. They need challenging, not chaperoning.

By the way, this is a good place to share a related concern: seniors are God's agents to help teach and train the younger generations. If you question that statement, read Titus 2:1–8. We don't believe that "traditional" and "contemporary" worship services are biblical or even necessary. The church is a family, and no matter what our ages we must learn to worship together. But the service must be balanced—"psalms, hymns and spiritual songs" (Eph. 5:19; Col. 3:16). The separated services not only segregate generations that ought to minister to each other, but they also divide families when children and parents ought to be worshiping together.

When it comes to evangelism, we may need different approaches to these generations. But Christian people ought to be able to worship together regardless of age, provided the service is balanced and carefully prepared.

WE HEAR A GREAT DEAL ABOUT "SUPPORT GROUPS," ESPECIALLY FOR PEOPLE WHO HAVE BEEN ABUSED OR NEED SPECIAL HELP. IS THIS AN OPPORTUNITY FOR THE CHURCH?

It can be, if you have people adequately trained to lead them. There are people in almost every church who carry painful secrets and hidden wounds and who need real encouragement. The loving ministry of the Word can help people forgive and forget. That's where healing begins, so don't minimize your preaching and teaching ministry. To set aside your Bible and pick up the latest psychology book is to take a step backward.

Whether or not your church should organize support groups depends on several factors. Do you have capable people to help lead them? Are there enough victims of abuse wanting help to warrant their getting together regularly, or would personal counseling work better? Will the groups be appendages to the church or will they be the church ministering? Is your church family willing to have the facilities used by outsiders who may treat them like a clubhouse?

Not everybody who attends a support group wants spiritual input; in fact, some of them are angry at the church. But this can be an opportunity for mature leaders to help them get a new perspective on the Lord and his people.

While the pastor ought to be in touch with each group, he probably shouldn't lead any of them unless the need is great and there is nobody else available. If you decide to direct a group, do your best to prepare for it. Maybe you can attend a seminar, and there are plenty of books available for you to study. Don't act like an amateur psychiatrist. The people to whom you'll be ministering need Christ before they need analysis.

Even if you don't start support groups, let it be known by your pastoral attitude and your preaching that you are aware of these hidden needs and you are willing to help. Keep your sense of humor under control and don't tell jokes about drunks, obese people, the mentally ill, or the divorced. Never say anything that could stab the heart of an abuse victim or an addict.

Even though they may not know the personal secrets of everybody who attends, the entire church ought to be a support group for those who hurt. By your example and teaching, help your people show compassionate understanding and Christlike care. Rejected and unwanted people felt at home in the presence of God's Son (Luke 15:1), and they should feel at home with God's people. Perhaps you could start a group for parents who have experienced the death of a child, or people who are recently divorced. Their wounds are deep and won't heal quickly.

I'VE READ REPORTS THAT THE AMERICAN FAMILY STRUCTURE IS CHANGING AND THAT THE CHURCH NEEDS TO ADAPT TO THESE CHANGES. IN WHAT WAYS?

Social institutions are always changing, but in recent years the changes in the American family have been dramatic. Not all of these changes are good, but all of them are attempts at survival.

The traditional nuclear family—a married couple caring for their children—is being challenged by other arrangements. The prevalence of divorce means that many children may live only with the father or the mother, or perhaps with another relative. Many single mothers must be both homemakers and breadwinners, and this is a challenge. We even have "blended families" as a result of divorce and remarriage, and "same-sex marriages" and other arrangements that we may not endorse but we still must help people cope with.

Again, this isn't a field for amateurs, so do some investigating before you invite people to come in. A single-parents' fellowship can give added support, but be sure you structure it in such a way that you don't rob the parents of the times they need with their children. You'll have to provide free child care for some who may not be able to afford babysitters. There are pros and cons about a single-parent Sunday school class, so consult with people who've done it and know the problems. Some single parents want to study the Bible with their peers, married or single, and not just with people who have the same burdens they do. However, a weeknight fellowship seems to work successfully. Our main job is to introduce them to Jesus Christ and encourage them in their spiritual growth.

While it's good for you to stay abreast of social trends, keep in mind that the church ministers to real people and not to statistical abstractions. If there are segments of the population that your church's ministry is neglecting, study the matter and see what the Lord might want you to do. But avoid becoming the religious ringmaster of a church circus. If the Lord doesn't provide leadership for these specialized ministries, wait and pray and give him time to work. Remember Acts 6:4 and the priority of prayer and the Word of God.

I REALLY FEEL INTIMIDATED WHEN I READ ABOUT SUPERCHURCHES, AND I WONDER IF THERE'S SOMETHING WRONG WITH ME OR MY MINISTRY. ANY SUGGESTIONS?

The average local church in America has about one hundred people attending, and God is able to use these churches to witness and minister. He isn't limited by the many or the few. Here and there, you will find megachurches that have experienced unbelievable growth and whose ministries are being imitated by other churches, but not always successfully.

Too many Christians think small and really don't want their churches to grow, and this is wrong. The fact that a church is large is no evidence that it isn't spiritual. However, to only think big and to use every gimmick available to get big crowds is also a mistake.

The church that really wants to grow to the glory of God (and not just for the reputation of the preacher) must prepare for growth. Suppose the Lord did give you scores or hundreds of new Christians in the next few months. Are you prepared to receive them and nurture them? Could your local body successfully assimilate that many people? A church of three hundred people is not only bigger than a church of seventy-five people, but it is radically different. A larger church must be organized and operated in an entirely different way from the smaller church. Are your leaders prepared to make these drastic changes?

Some of today's megachurches were founded by their current pastors and therefore nurtured the way they felt God wanted the church to grow. It's one thing to give birth to a giant and quite something else to turn an old pygmy into a young giant. It can be done, but there's a price to pay. Sometimes you have to clean house and start the ministry all over again, and this is painful. Better that we allow the church to give birth to a new and different church and not get the reputation of causing a church split.

If you're faithfully doing the work God has called you to do, and he's blessing your ministry, never feel intimidated by what's happening in other churches (John 3:26–30). Give thanks for what God is doing in other churches and in your church, because if one part of the body is strengthened, the whole body is strengthened; so all of us are enriched. Churches, like children, are all different and grow at different rates. Nurture the people God has given you and keep your eyes on the work he wants you to do.

Never borrow somebody's methods until you understand the principles behind them and agree with them. Imitation is no guarantee of success. The church that meets the needs of people, that leads them into a deepening experience of worship and service, and that organizes and prepares for growth, trusting God for his blessing, will surely enjoy the blessing of God as he sees fit to bless.

The Scottish writer George MacDonald said, "In whatever man does without God, he must fail miserably, or succeed more miserably." Our Lord wants us to have fruit, more fruit, much fruit

(John 15:2, 5, 8), but he warns us that "apart from me you can do nothing" (John 15:5). In today's world, it doesn't take much to gather a crowd, but it takes a great deal to build a church. An old poem says,

> Methods are many, principles are few;
> Methods always change; principles never do.

Stick to biblical principles and don't be an imitator.
Be an original.

The Word at Work Around the World

A vital part of Cook Communications Ministries is our international outreach, Cook Communications Ministries International (CCMI). Your purchase of this book, and of other books and Christian-growth products from Cook, enables CCMI to provide Bibles and Christian literature to people in more than 150 languages in 65 countries.

Cook Communications Ministries is a not-for-profit, self-supporting organization. Revenues from sales of our books, Bible curricula, and other church and home products not only fund our U.S. ministry, but also fund our CCMI ministry around the world. One hundred percent of donations to CCMI go to our international literature programs.

CCMI reaches out internationally in three ways:

· Our premier International Christian Publishing Institute (ICPI) trains leaders from nationally led publishing houses around the world.

· We provide literature for pastors, evangelists, and Christian workers in their national language.

· We reach people at risk—refugees, AIDS victims, street children, and famine victims—with God's Word.

Word Power, God's Power

Faith Kidz, RiverOak, Honor, Life Journey, Victor, NexGen — every time you purchase a book produced by Cook Communications Ministries, you not only meet a vital personal need in your life or in the life of someone you love, but you're also a part of ministering to José in Colombia, Humberto in Chile, Gousa in India, or Lidiane in Brazil. You help make it possible for a pastor in China, a child in Peru, or a mother in West Africa to enjoy a life-changing book. And because you helped, children and adults around the world are learning God's Word and walking in his ways.

Thank you for your partnership in helping to disciple the world. May God bless you with the power of his Word in your life.

For more information about our international ministries, visit www.ccmi.org.

Additional copies of *Pastors' FAQs*
and other NexGen titles are available
from your local bookseller.

If you have enjoyed this book,
or if it has had an impact on your life,
we would like to hear from you.

Please contact us at:

NexGen Books
Cook Communications Ministries, Dept. 201
4050 Lee Vance View
Colorado Springs, CO 80918
Or visit our Web site: www.cookministries.com

Building the New Generation of Believers